HOW MORAL
PHILOSOPHY
BROKE POLITICS

AND

HOW TO FIX IT

Robert A Johnson

Published in 2022 by Ockham Publishing in the United Kingdom

ISBN 978-1-83919-030-8

Cover design by Claire Wood

www.ockham-publishing.com

About the author

Robert A Johnson is a practical ethicist and philosopher of science, who graduated in Mental Philosophy from the University of Aberdeen. He specialises in the intersection of morality and rationality, whilst being a staunch advocate of science and evidence-based endeavours. His other interests and work lie primarily in animal ethics, where he has written numerous articles on animal welfare and animal rights, whilst standing up for non-human interests from a rational perspective.

www.robertjohnson.org.uk

Facebook @RationalMorality

Twitter @robjohnson86

Contents

Introduction

Politics seems to be in crisis, in every conceivable way. In a 2019 audit on the UK's opinion on politics, the Hansard Society discovered:

"72% say the system of governing needs 'quite a lot' or 'a great deal' of improvement."

"75% say the main political parties are so divided within themselves that they cannot serve the best interests of the country."

"63% think Britain's system of government is rigged to advantage the rich and powerful."

"50% say the main parties and politicians don't care about people like them."

"[When] asked whether the problem is the system or the people, the largest group (38%) say 'both'."[1]

This issue is not unique to Britain, either. According to Pew research, 82% of Americans do not think that the political system is working very well, while 61% say "significant changes" are needed in the fundamental "design and structure" of the US government to make it fit for the modern world.[2]

Across Europe the story is similar: people are worried about how fit for purpose big political institutions are, even within the institutions that people most respect. In every member of the EU, except for Spain,

---

[1]https://www.hansardsociety.org.uk/publications/reports/audit-of-political-engagement-16
[2] https://www.pewresearch.org/topics/trust-facts-and-democracy/

the majority of voters believe it is possible that the EU will fall apart in the next 10-20 years, despite two thirds of all those polled believing that the EU has been positive for their country.

These views are repeated time and again, throughout the individual EU countries within their own governments. Only around 7% of French people, for example, trust their political parties (and only 14% trust the national government)[3]. Indeed, as seeming anomalies, only Germany, the Netherlands and Sweden's electorates have net positive views of their political parties within Europe; yet even the most impressive, in Germany, only garner between 58% and 68% approval in doing so. An anomaly, perhaps, but still not hugely impressive scoring, when between one third and two fifths of the population are unhappy.[4]

Opinions in Asia are harder to come across, in terms of accurate polling, both because of differences in political systems but also because of the limits of free speech and media in countries such as China and North Korea. According to the Democracy Index, Asia has a far higher proportion of authoritarian and flawed democracies[5], so honest assessments of governments there are difficult. But countries such as Japan (9%), South Korea (12%), Taiwan (14%), Mongolia (17%), the Philippines and Thailand (both 35%) and Indonesia (42%) all share in having a majority of voters distrusting political parties.[6] When asked about the question of trust in parliament itself, the answers are similar (though Indonesia just rises to 50%).

---

[3] https://ec.europa.eu/commfrontoffice/publicopinion/archives/eb/eb80/eb80_fr_fr_nat.pdf

[4] https://www.pewresearch.org/global/2017/06/15/few-political-parties-in-europe-have-widespread-appeal/

[5] https://www.eiu.com/topic/democracy-index

[6] http://asianbarometer.org/publications//e7d4c03698433c4a579ca0132bd28898.pdf

Where confidence in government remains over 50%, in Asia or elsewhere, we are still seeing drops. India polled at over 80% in 2007 but dropped to around 55% by 2012. In the same time period South Africa dropped from around 67% to just under 50%.[7] So whilst 50% or more sounds successful compared to the UK or the US, the drops can be astounding.

Within Africa, again we have difficulties assessing these same questions for the same reason as it is difficult in Asia: lots of countries score low on the democracy index, so people could be killed for expressing distrust in government. But even then there is still evidence of distrust and unhappiness in politics: a cross-national comparative of 18 African countries appears to show that at least 7 hold populations where 50% or more distrust parliament.[8]

Finally, what about the sunny climates of Australia? Or the snowy wonderland of Canada? The Social Research Institute at Ipsos, in July 2018, showed Australians' trust in politicians and democracy hit an all-time low: 31% and 40.6% respectively.[9] Trust for political parties was at just 16%. In Canada, according to an Angus Reid Institute poll in 2019, only 28% of people appear to trust politicians.[10]

Whilst we feel this distrust and lack of hope in our governments and our politicians, these statistics show that it is not just us, but widespread throughout the world.

---

[7]https://www.oecd-ilibrary.org/docserver/gov_glance-2013-6-en.pdf?expires=1574505954&id=id&accname=guest&checksum=B844D7B98959C84C04A2343F9B7066F5

[8]https://afrobarometer.org/sites/default/files/publications/Policy%20paper/AfropaperNo84.pdf

[9]https://www.democracy2025.gov.au/documents/Democracy2025-report1.pdf

[10] http://angusreid.org/views-of-politicians/

Lack of hope rather than revolution?

In history, when we see large numbers of people unhappy with their government, we tend to witness revolutions and coups rather than simple unhappiness and hopelessness. So why is it only in places such as Syria, where people are overthrowing authoritarian regimes, that we are seeing this?

The answer appears to be in a Pew Research global attitudes survey from 2017[11], in which it showed that 78% and 66% believe respectively that representative or direct democracies are a good way of governing their country. People don't trust politics, and they don't appear to think the system of government works either, but those of us who live in democracies tend to think it's better than the alternatives. After all, we need our leaders to be accountable to the voters, or else government is opened up to all kinds of levels of human bias, military coups, corruption and personal gain.

As a result, we harbour distrust and lack hope, but our governments largely continue unchallenged as we believe this is the best there is.

Why does a previous failure within moral philosophy hold the key?

The UK is a good example of one of the many political systems globally that hasn't massively changed in hundreds of years: with our odd traditions and quirks, where mostly everyone votes for one of two dogmatic parties who call each other 'honourable gentlemen' one day and

---

[11]https://www.pewresearch.org/global/2017/10/16/globally-broad-support-for-representative-and-direct-democracy/

'terrorist sympathiser' the next, all the while our media takes sides or else believes centrism is neutrality.

Yet, whilst politics hasn't changed much, the world has evolved rapidly around it. Far from a world in which we burn people at the stake for being witches, we can now fly people to the moon, fly automated robots to explore Mars, create huge skyscrapers, harvest data about people in their millions, create quantum computers and vaccinate against illnesses that previously killed millions. We can call friends and colleagues who are thousands of miles away, and speak to them via video chat in seconds. The world has changed drastically – some might say unimaginably – but our idea of what democratic politics involves hasn't, which has left it incapable in the modern world.

The reason underpinning that stagnation is unbelievably simple yet largely unknown, and stems from a basic, yet logical, philosophical principle popularised by David Hume: the is-ought problem.

Put simply, the is-ought problem states that the way things are do not justify the way things should be. Simple, elegant, and almost certainly true. So, an 'is' (the way something 'is') shouldn't create an 'ought' (the way something 'ought' to be).

But it means that whilst science and technology have massively revolutionised the world, and society as a whole – by increasing our objective knowledge of what 'is' – our politics remains entirely separate, and entirely subjective, as it is predicated on the world of 'oughts'.

A good example of this is climate change. Scientists have proved, without any real doubt, that human-caused climate change exists. They've also developed knowledge of what causes it, what slows it down and even how we can reverse some of it. They've gone so far as to give us rough ideas, even, of what we need to do – reducing carbon emissions – and by at what point in order to avoid catastrophic temperature increases. Science has identified the problem, how to stop it and what we can do.

But because we all believe our moral opinions are subjective, unwittingly due to our belief in the is-ought problem, our politics are predicated in a way that reflects this. So politicians are provided the facts, and in most Western countries even agree with them, but develop political perspectives (or, in other words, moral opinions) to shield themselves from having to take the facts on board. Whilst some countries have perspectives that allow them to accept the facts and act. And furthermore, such as in the USA, some governments entirely doubt that science actually exists, and so presumably just pretend society hasn't advanced due to science.

And climate change is just one area – politicians do this on everything. In most countries the split is between left and right, whereby the left tends to want to fund social and health care services, but distrust science in some shocking ways, and the right tends to want to allow capitalism to solve issues, and reduce the size of the state. Or, in countries like the UK, there is often also a centrist choice, which is a mishmash of the two. At no point can there be a rationalist party because we believe that morality is subjective and not rational, so how can we have a rationalist perspective in politics? With this in mind, the political see-saw, changing every four, eight or twelve years based on elections, from one dogma to the next, seems inevitable.

Inevitable, that is, unless we can find a way around the is-ought problem, and come up with a rational, justifiable way to judge moral opinions, and thus base politics and economics on reason. Something which makes sense, takes into account different opinions and – more to the point – doesn't violate that principle that Hume rightly defined all those years ago.

Hope is possible

In the last 15 years, at least in the US and the UK, we have only heard the word 'hope' in politics when it is said in relation to particular political positions. Obama offered 'hope' to democrats, in that he could get elected, and Corbyn offered 'hope' to Labour, in that he wanted to oust the Tories. However, real hope isn't found in delighting one group of people at the expense of another, but rather in uniting all behind a common cause – something new, inspiring and untested – and in allowing politics to evolve into the modern world, rather than be so far behind it.

Particularly in the UK, though undoubtedly around the world, society is split between left and right. Referendums go further and simply leave entire societies divided on wanting the country to be run based on different dogmas. This can't be the best way, and I aim to show that it isn't the best way. Just as science and reason has jumped society forwards over the last 200 years, the same methodology can do so for politics.

This, in political campaigns, is where the author, blogger, journalist, politician or activist would normally ask you to *believe* in the change they want to offer you. And that's where this is different. You don't have to believe it, because it's based on reason. You can read and follow the logical progression. You can read it and agree with it, or you can read it and disagree with it, but it offers you reason as to why and how things could be different. Not just a different political persuasion, an entirely different system. One that works, is still accountable to the voters, but is modern, based in reason, philosophically justified and rationally progressive.

Structure

Politicians are often told to 'finish with a flourish', hence why you can find numerous examples of them getting a verbal beating during debates, sounding as clueless as you can imagine, yet still trying to reel off a series of pre-prepared soundbites as they sum up at the end. Like a robot who hasn't quite grasped the situation they're actually in. As if to prove that this isn't the normal way of doing this, the end to this introduction is instead a guide in how this book works.

I've talked a lot above about why this idea is important. It's not miraculous, it's not historic, it's just reason, and it's necessary. So the first part of the book has to deal with the reason and philosophy itself. Chapters 1 – 4 are thus about discovering what the problems are, how to create a rational version of morality, what it entails and roughly how it would practically work. Chapters 5 – 7 give some basic guidance on how a rational, consensus-based moral code would affect some big areas (such as determinism and animal ethics) before we get to politics. Chapters 8 and 9 are where we really get to the crux of how we can develop a rational, effective and flourishing form of accountable government and economics, having solved the is-ought problem.

Chapter 1: Marrying Morality with Reality

How do we decide what's right and wrong?

In 2012 a prominent politician (one of the most influential decision makers in Britain[12]) published a much-referenced article in a British newspaper entitled 'We stand side by side with the Pope in fighting for faith'.[13] In it, Baroness Warsi noted that Europe needs to be "more confident and more comfortable in its Christianity" and warns against "militant secularisation" which "demonstrates similar traits to totalitarian regimes".

One might be puzzled by such statements; after all Britain doesn't seem overly "militant" in its secularism.[14] There's no one burning down churches or mosques in the name of atheism, for example, and those who most militantly advocate secularism seem to do so with no more aggression than to speak or write about it. Quite a long way from

---

[12] At the time, the politician in question was both a cabinet minister – which is one of the primary people consulted on UK government decisions and policy – and co-chairman of the ruling party.

[13]   http://www.telegraph.co.uk/news/religion/9080441/We-stand-side-by-side-with-the-Pope-in-fighting-for-faith.html

[14] Then Prime Minister, David Cameron, himself issued pro-religious sentiments in 2011, claiming that the UK is a Christian country and "should not be afraid to say so" (http://www.bbc.co.uk/news/uk-politics-16224394). If nothing else, this shows that Britain is far from militant in its secularism – the head of state himself pushes the idea of the state as religious, not secular.

totalitarian regimes, one might argue. Indeed, since 2012 the world has seen an increase in religious extremism – cities as diverse as Paris, London, Ankara and Boston have suffered horrific attacks. It seems naive to note that many of the recent attacks were Islamic, and so to argue that Christianity is valuable whilst Islam is destructive. A quick glance through history would not allow Christianity off the hook; perhaps a modern look at American terrorism, and its many shootings related to Christian delusions, would also rebalance the scales. And that's before we talk about the violent opposition we see towards abortion clinics.

People have naturally waned from Christianity over the years, undoubtedly, but militant secularism seems like an overstatement. This natural move towards secularisation is even understandable. There's no evidence for untestable assertions like that of a God, and people seem to have naturally recognised that religion might just be wishful thinking. The late Christopher Hitchens perhaps summarised it best when he wrote that "I was educated by Sir Karl Popper to believe that a theory that is unfalsifiable is to that extent a weak one."[15] To posit assertions about creators of the universe is akin to positing assertions about surely mythical guardians of the galaxy – the evidence that supports Rocket Raccoon or He-Man being our real saviour is equal to that of God.

Warsi's entire article seems a bit odd, that is until you read her justification for making such statements: "To create a more just society, people need to feel stronger in their religious identities and more confident in their creeds."

---

[15] Quoted in *God is Not Great*. Hitchens is referring to the work of the great philosopher of science, Karl Popper, whose work is still a guiding influence in defending and promoting the reasons why science is such a wonderful method of truth finding.

Unwittingly, in an impassioned defence of religion, Warsi places her finger right on the pulse of what is arguably the biggest innate problem we face as a society and as a species. With the ever-increasing secularisation of society, stemming from an entirely reasonable rejection of religion, there also seems to be an air of moral confusion. It pours from the gap left by our previous moral rule bearer of religion, and seems to ask us to conclude that without God to set the rules, morality must be flexible and relative else non-existent.[16]

As such, society is facing a crisis of confusion when it comes to moral inclinations. On the one hand, we want to oppose murder, rape, and hundreds of other heinous acts of cruelty which are currently against the law, in the most fundamental manner. The media and our personal opinions are still outraged by these kinds of acts against innocent victims. On the other hand, we seem to be in a position of

---

[16] One study that show this in particular, http://onthehuman.org/2010/12/objective-moral-truths/. Knobe notes that there is no evidence to show that people believe morality to be objective, and explains various studies on the subject which show that several types of people tend toward moral relativism. Most interestingly, when discussing Feltz and Cokely: "they conducted a study in which they measured both openness to experience and belief in moral relativism...The higher a participant was in openness to experience, the more likely that participant was to give a relativist answer."

Knobe discusses similar findings from Goodwin and Darley which showed that people who consider a variety of possibilities in answering questions are also more inclined to offer relativist answers.

These two studies heavily support the idea that people who are more open to experience, or more open to other views, show an inclination to moral relativism. This backs up common sense, as our moral rules are built upon Abrahamic religious foundations, and so when people begin shedding this as the sole acceptable viewpoint, they tend toward a more accepting view of other types. Hence they tend toward moral relativism. This backs up my point that as society becomes more secular, rightly or wrongly it tends toward moral relativism.

understanding that morality is largely relative and thus any newly thought moral or immoral acts we see people engaging in (ethical veganism as moral, or deforestation as immoral, for example) are a matter of subjective choice rather than of any sense right or wrong.[17] We tend to take the position that what is illegal is wrong, but so long as something is legal it is acceptable, and thereby only to be taken as immoral in relation to personal tastes. Law reflects objective wrongs, whilst all others are subjective.

This creates a paradoxical tension, an infinite feedback loop that wasn't there before, as law itself is primarily a reflection of our majority societal opinions. So if we want to oppose something that's against the law then we need to be able justify why we oppose it – *we make law, it doesn't make itself* – and similarly we need to leave the law open for new things which we discover to be immoral, in order to legally forbid them. But how can we do this if we want to claim that doing right or wrong is just a choice? How can we believe that morality is both objective and subjective: that some things are wrong, yet others of the same ferocity are a matter of choice? To understand the issue more completely, we need to explore the topics involved.

Law as a reflection of social opinion

There is no 'all seeing eye' who creates and maintains the juridical system. In modern democratic systems, laws are invented and amended

---

[17] Of course, one would have to agree veganism was a coherent, rational moral choice in the first place – a claim doubted by both some of those in favour of animal rights and those against it. And also that deforestation is immoral. However, here I use them as examples, as people often put these down to a notion of "each to their own" rather than a matter of right and wrong. We don't do this with things like murder, or rape, so it is interesting that we feel the need to do it with moral issues that are not illegal.

by us. This simple observation quashes the idea that something being against the law makes it immoral, or that something being perfectly legal makes it acceptable. As history progresses, laws will change, and they thus reflect societal opinion of the time, rather than the ultimate answer on whether an act is morally right or wrong.

The most popular examples to demonstrate this point often focus on human slavery, or other things we now find morally abhorrent but which a few hundred years ago may have been perfectly legal. In fact, one may not be far wrong in claiming everything we now view as immoral would have been legal somewhere, at some point in history (race-based slavery, or the ownership of women are good examples). And, unsurprisingly, many things we now find acceptable or even moral (such as challenging scientific conclusions with new evidence or criticising religious doctrine by pointing to its inherent paradoxes or lack of evidence) would have been deemed morally unacceptable in some society at some point. Law is merely the reflection of the current societal attitudes and cannot be used as justification for moral stances, at least not any more than we can justify them by saying that we *can* physically commit said acts. This statement is summed up nicely by the phrase *'the way things are does not justify the way they ought to be'*. I *could* jump out of my second-floor window right now, and likely break a bone or two, but this does not imply that I *should*. The laws of physics and the laws of the land share in *allowing* us to commit ourselves to certain actions, but neither could be taken as sole *moral justification* for doing so.

The most likely explanation for the widespread belief in current moral norms, and the corresponding offering of moral guidance solely to law, was uncovered by Eidelman et al in a study called The Existence

Bias.[18] The authors demonstrated that "people treat the mere existence of something as evidence of its goodness...the status quo is seen as good, right...and desirable." Studies such as this can explain why our problematic and irrational beliefs formed, but if the status quo does not conclusively tell us what is acceptable and what is wrong, then what does? The natural act is to begin applying scepticism to the subject of morality.

Does morality even exist?

Religious justification

The oldest and arguably still the most popular reason for invoking a notion of morality is down to religion. If God exists, and has rules he wants us to follow, then these are moral facts. We can thus judge the wrongness or acceptability of any action with reference to whether God approves or not.

Society increasingly rejects this form of moral theory though, with Western society (and indeed various states within Africa and Asia) now providing examples of almost entirely secular governments.[19] We live

---

[18] The Existence Bias. *Journal of Personality and Social Psychology 2009*, Vol. 97, No. 5, 765-775. Eidelman, S., Pattershall, J. and Crandall, C.S.

[19] We hear many examples of this: Sweden, Netherlands and an increasing number of non-European countries around the world claim to be secular (it is difficult to measure just how many states are truly secular in approach). The most interesting case of secularisation in government is in Honduras, where the following guarantee of religious separation from government can be found in Article 77 of the constitution (translated): "It guarantees the free exercise of all religions and cults without precedence, provided they do not contravene the laws and public order. The ministers of different religions, may not hold public office or engage in any form of political propaganda, on grounds of religion or using as a means to that end of the religious beliefs of the people." One wonders how different political campaigns in hugely influential countries like the US would look with this kind of approach.

in a world where science moves us forward and is valued based on the fact that it needs to *demonstrate* (or at least conclusively and rationally imply) that which it wants to confirm as true, rather than merely announcing it. So when such an excellent and developed system for finding truth exists, why would we use the justification of something which we have no evidence for at all? One by one we have discarded beliefs formed out of myth and tradition. The most notable remaining myth in society is religion and its gods.

There is no relevance in the 21st century to an argument that says *'A force/man which I have no evidence for, and which I believe in simply because of my own personal valuing of a mental occurrence called faith, should tell me what to do. My proof is that it is written in a book'*. We should respect religious *people* as much as we can within society, but if we take issues like morality seriously we should not be subjecting it to ideas for which there is no evidence. God may be a more serious concept for people than the Flying Spaghetti Monster,[20] but when we are discussing rationally they should share equal, non-existent pull. Similarly, opinions about 'forces' or 'energies' which do not resemble classic ideas of God, but which claim to provide moral ideas (like karma, for instance) should be tested and subjected to the rigours of reason. A scientist would be rightly ignored, and perhaps even laughed out of conferences for stating that gravity is not a justifiable force, but that we're attracted to the ground because strong, invisible, prehistoric jelly covers the earth's surface. And yet religious and spiritual ideas, like the existence of God, or karma, hold the same level of evidence. Advancement is about proving past ideas wrong, or discarding them based on

---

[20] http://www.venganza.org/

what we now know, in order to develop our knowledge base. But if we can't discard something there's zero evidence for, then there's little point in trying to discard anything and the whole system suffers a major flaw.

The 'science is also faith-based' defence

It is true that not every piece of scientific knowledge we have can be conclusively supported; indeed theoretical science deals with ideas which we may as yet have no evidence to test with. However, every one of these 'theories' are required because we know there must be *a* theory. Take quantum mechanics, where several theories battle for describing several different concepts, which we have as yet been unable to conclusively test – at least not to a level of satisfactory and conclusive results (though, we appear to get closer every year). Even if we were never able to test them, we still know that there must be *a* theory that is correct, as we see activity that must work based on some law. Thus there is need to devise a theory that explains it. However, ideas like religion are not theories in the same manner. We have no need to imply that a theory of religion is needed, as the universe looks precisely as it should look were there to be no God, and were we to be individuals without a perfect ability to understand how the universe works.

If we could say the same about physics at the quantum level – that it looks precisely how it should look if there were no quantum theories – then quantum theory would be a mute subject and would not be considered science. We see subatomic particles appear to behave in ways we need explanation for, though, so we create theories of explanation to test. We have never come across an event with which we need to create a theory of God to explain – not when we have the ability to say 'we don't know how that happens yet' – and furthermore, what kind of idea could have us so perplexed, that culturally invented icons and mythologies are a good explanation? It is best to remember that God was created in human minds; there is no evidence for it, and we've no need to invoke a theory of God in order to explain worldly events.

If you have to use God as an explanation for something then all kinds of other ideas are back on the table also: Thor, Allah, Superman, the Flying Spaghetti Monster, Spider-Man, an omnipotent Barbie or an all-seeing alien cockroach are just a tiny fraction of an infinite number of explanations that work as well as a theory of God. It is only when you consider the sheer number of other potential theories which work just as well as God, in the situations where God could possibly be required as an explanation, that you realise just how poor an explanation it is. If there is something we can't explain then a cultural myth is not likely to be the answer we are searching for. 'Randomness' or 'chance' is actually always going to be a better explanation than 'God', as it is always more likely that things happen entirely naturally but in a way we can't fathom yet, than it is that they happen because an omnipotent and immaterial being created them.

As a result of ideas like this, and given the ever increasing secularisation of society over the years, we've begun to grow away from these irrational religious ideals of morality as a factual, God-given concept. Previously, many societies were largely ruled by the idea that a God or benevolent force had set the rules and we must follow them, else we might be punished in some way.[21] Many Western court rooms, which

---

[21] Believed punishments would vary depending on the society – examples include Karmic rebuttals within your own life, or an afterlife justice like heaven and hell depending on the society.

dealt with such laws here on Earth, started proceedings with oaths on the Bible.[22] However, as science has gotten more capable, so has our ability to doubt the existence of a Creator of any kind.

The rational debunking of this first aspect, religion, has left morality in the firing line. Religion is the easiest way to justify morality, as it claims to need no evidence. So if there is no God setting moral rules, how do such rules realistically exist in the first place? After all, scientists are hardly climbing mountains to uncover new moral facts underneath rocks, or implying the existence of moral truths in reactions after the collision of particles at a sub-atomic level. If God isn't setting objective moral laws, how do they exist?

The spiritual 'get out clause'?

It's true that many admit the fallibility of religious conceptions of morality in modern society; however, a good chunk of those people believe there is an irrational 'get out clause' in science, which means spiritual arguments are valid, and thereby we can base our morality around what would have been irrational ideas like 'independent moral facts'.[23] With a regular reference to quantum mechanics (an area of science that proves very popular in religious and spiritual discussions due to it being fundamentally misunderstood by many), the argument goes that some areas of science conclusively prove that the laws of physics are

---

[22] A practice continued to this day in countries like the USA.

[23] An 'independent moral fact' is my way of referencing the idea that a moral fact exists in the same way a physics or biology fact does – people who believe in 'independent moral facts' (primarily known as 'moral realists') believe that these facts exist out with human society, and are facts that we are simply uncovering. They believe that our intuitions or calculations or logic can uncover these pre-existing facts, in the same way that we can uncover facts in science through investigation.

paradoxical. Hence we do not know science to be a reliable, consistent method, and spiritual ideas are perfectly valid.

Indeed quantum mechanics is an interesting modern form of scientific investigation, which baffled (and still baffles) many physicists. Danish physicist Niels Bohr famously said, "Anyone who is not shocked by quantum theory has not understood it." Whilst the infamous Richard Feynman is thought to have elaborated further with, "If you think you understand quantum mechanics, you don't understand quantum mechanics."[24] It's little wonder that people have leapt on the subject in order to provide evidence for the mysterious. It's not at all difficult to find spiritual groups and influenced companies who mangle the ideas or terminology of quantum mechanics in order to make a profit or create a justification for nonsense.[25]

Quantum mechanics truly is a fascinating discipline, and not just because of its counter-intuitive results. The entire area demonstrates the real strengths of science: that whatever ideas are held to be correct should be constantly challenged if new evidence is uncovered. Science does not stick to rigid accounts of events which do not hold to be true,

---

[24] Bohr As quoted in *Meeting the Universe Halfway* (2007) by Karen Michelle Barad, p. 254, with a footnote citing *The Philosophical Writings of Niels Bohr* (1998). No-one can be certain that Feynman stated his attributed quote, although many people attest that it was definitely his style! In any case, the quote is an interesting one.

[25] Primarily those making profit tend to exploit the 'quantum healing' phenomenon, for which even the community run Wikipedia defines as a "pseudo-scientific mixture of ideas drawing on quantum mechanics..." (http://en.wikipedia.org/wiki/Quantum_healing)
Those working in ethics use and abuse quantum mechanics in all kind of ways, and in debates I have variously encountered it as being used in a circular attempt to disprove determinism (and hence show that any rational argument against independent moral facts is flawed by virtue of relying on rationality as a marker of truth).

and instead develops as our understanding of the world develops. Quantum mechanics would not be studied under the umbrella of science at all if scientists were not held strictly to these high standards.

But what is either a dishonest claim or a simple misunderstanding is that areas like quantum mechanics mean spiritual 'theories' should be supported. Sure, science is a developing system which constantly evolves and so can often hold truths which it later proves to be wrong. But the truths it holds are not personally posited, nor the subject of desires, individual experiences or armchair philosophical inquiry. Every truth held in science (however wrong it may prove to be in the future) is held precisely because it makes sense with what we know of the world, and is the best account we have in relation to the evidence. A spiritual idea that says we can't prove everything with science, or that science is wrong by virtue of its evolution, is engaging in methodological hyperbole. Science is built to take into account the changing nature of truth based on increasing levels of evidence, so it is telling that it has yet to embrace the supernatural as having positive truth values.

The spiritualist will also often point at the 'big bang' and question "what came before it?" The answer science predicts of nothingness is not a shot in the dark so much as the best supported answer we have. There is no evidence that there was anything before the big bang, but there is evidence to suggest there was a big bang. The spiritualist who claims nothingness cannot create something (however intuitive this is) shouldn't then posit a spiritual idea, which there is no evidence for, as true due to this paradox about nothingness which they have identified.

The fact is that there is less evidence for any spiritual idea you can think of (whether it be of a supernatural force, or energy, the positions appear to be limitless) than there is for nothingness. The beauty of admitting there may have been nothing, but that science hasn't yet developed to a space where we can begin to answer these questions fully (possibly because the problem is our limits of understanding 'spacetime', rather than that the answer is paradoxical), is in the fact that we are being honest. The dishonesty of claiming it was a god, or a similarly irrational spiritual idea is clear to see. And as the example of the Flying Spaghetti Monster shows, it makes no sense to posit these equally unsupported spiritual ideas which claim to answer questions they couldn't possibly know the solution to. These responses are the equivalent of making answers up. If you can't figure out the answer to a mathematical problem, you don't just make an answer up. This might be a good bet if you want to maximise your chances on an exam, but a developing body of knowledge cannot work when it's filled with random or personal guesses.

The mathematics comparison

A popular, more rational (though still arguably spiritual) argument for asserting independent moral facts (moral facts which are there for us to investigate and uncover, and not created by humans or society) comes from comparing morality with other 'non-physical' concepts that we do think exist, like mathematics. If it is true that Pi = 3.14159265... (and so on), despite Pi not being a physical fact found under rocks or on mountains, then why can't it be true that murder is wrong? Both appear to be non-physical facts so why can't both have independent truth values? This, in a nutshell, is the argument that our intuitions about morality relate to moral facts in the same way that our intuitions about mathematics relate to mathematical facts. This is clearly a step up in logic from the basic arguments we just discussed.

13

The comparison, though compelling at first glance, is still illegitimate upon inquiry. Rational concepts, like mathematics, which are not rooted directly in physical facts about the world, stem from our understanding and investigated evidence in it. For example, the sum 2+2=4 is essentially linguistic symbolism for seeing two things, and adding that same amount of things again, so as we can symbolise the resulting amount (4) in our communication rather than having to be experiencing it at the time. No matter how complex and abstract mathematics can get, and no matter how removed from the world it can seem, you can always reduce any mathematical problem back to these initial observations if you really put in the effort. There is a real-world relation that supports the notion of 2+2=4, and the symbolic substitution of language is referencing it, not referencing some intuitive and non-physical concept. Maths is a symbolic way to explain real-world events, in ever-increasing complexity, for the furtherance of human understanding, without the inconvenience of having to get a million things and add a million things to it, to show the resulting 'two million', for example. It works for every form of maths when it is related back. Maths is a shorthand for real objects and measurements.

What about the most theoretical numbers, like Pi? They are still remarkably easy to draw back to real-world evidence. For example, Pi is infinite in digits, and we'll likely never know every last digit which it constitutes.[26] However, this does not mean our belief in Pi is abstract like our belief in moral facts would be. Pi represents a very real concept,

---

[26] We can't know every number of Pi without significant answers as to the problems with paradoxes, anyway – infinity has to end somewhere, doesn't it?! Well no, but there's no saying that rational inquiry cannot solve the problems with paradoxes which are currently posed and provide some finite figure for Pi, theoretically.

and we know it must exist from observations about Euclidean circles and the relation of their circumference to their diameter. It is a fact that Pi, as a concept, exists, and if you reduce it back to where it is being implied into existence, then you come back to those millions of measurements of circles made during the history of human civilisation. These measurements themselves are made with rulers, measured out and marked by numbers in a certain order; the order of the numbers being those same things which are symbolically referencing real-world objects (which we know exist from observing 2 stones + 2 stones, and referring to those 2 sets of 2 as 4, which in turn tells us the order of 1, 2, 3, 4, etc.). Like words creating sentences, we create mathematical arguments with symbols, but they reference real, physical facts if reduced back – like with any words. And hence the meaning of words and numbers are factual, being grounded in the materialist, scientific world.

So, mathematic intuitions do not exist out with the physical world; they are, however indirectly, informed by observations at every point, and can often be proved correct or incorrect. But how can the same thing be said of moral intuitions? These are intuitions implanted in us by a rich evolutionary history. They didn't evolve when the concept of God was invented, and this is supported by the fact that we see altruistic behaviour in other species,[27] and also by the existence of mirror neurons, which will be explained later on. And furthermore, given that everything we do is possible because of evolutionary development (morality is no different), then what makes moral facts a true concept, but

---

[27] Proof which should be strongly referenced, unless one wants to argue that other animals inherently believe in God and act morally as a result of this. A hypothesis one would struggle to find any support for.

15

not religious facts? Or colour facts? One could imply the factuality of any concept by reference to the fact we have intuitions about it, and if one doesn't agree that there is a universal, independent fact of what is the 'universally best colour' then that casts serious doubt on the consistency of arguing that there are acts which violate universal facts about morality. People's intuitions disagree on things as extremely immoral as murder, and hence we see people committing murder. So to pretend that intuitions tell us 'murder is wrong' is simply to push your own intuitions as correct rather than the murderer's, on the arbitrary basis that they aren't you, or perhaps that they aren't in agreement with the majority of you. If you disagree about mathematics, one of you can most likely be proved right with linguistic argumentation which draws back to real-world truths, or by physical experiment, whereas the same cannot be said about disagreements on morality, in which we could only ever push our own opinions.

So although mathematics might involve intuitions at some point (there might be an intuition to measure things, or a seemingly innate yet probably learned intuition that 4 is bigger than 3), they are of a very different type to morality. We can prove or disprove our mathematical inclinations by reference to facts in the world, and when they are so abstract as to defy current methods of proof (or even defy all methods of proof forevermore) we can at least go back and provide reasons why we think it is the case (reducing back to physical facts and noting the reasons why there must be a mathematical law which the numbers are adhering to). And indeed if a theory doesn't match up with the facts we can prove about mathematics, then we can discard it and remain in search of a better answer which might be the true fact on the issue. We can even be unsure if it is truly knowable.

But what happens if we hold morality to these same rigours that other non-physical facts (like mathematical facts) have to be held to? We can't even get started down this path, as morality isn't derived from evidence and facts like mathematics is. We can say someone is being murdered (a fact), and that we feel bad about it (a fact), but how can we say that it is right to feel bad about it because there is a universal fact that 'murder is wrong', which this emotion is referring to? Such a physical fact doesn't, and can't, exist. Moreover, if classic morality passes this test of reason by virtue of it relating to intuition, then so can any belief. Realistically speaking, the fact I feel things doesn't make it true that the feeling is correct, and similarly the fact I want something to be wrong doesn't make it wrong. This is the argument that flaws religious thought as a rational matter, and it also does away with the idea that there are independent moral facts that we can search for.

It seems fair to say the mathematics comparison is simply inaccurate, and if moral facts do exist they certainly aren't of the type that says intuition is referring to independent moral facts about the universe. We need a more relativist form of morality in order to marry it with reality, one which takes into account the fact that morality exists because evolution has developed it into us as a social tool, and which does not make claims about there being non-physical facts floating in the universe to which our intuitions can be right or wrong in relation to.

The evolution of morality

As touched upon in the last paragraph, morality is a socially evolved trait. In Richard Dawkins' update on Darwin's theory of evolution, *The Selfish Gene*,[28] he notes that our bodies are vehicles for genes which,

---

[28] *The Selfish Gene*, Richard Dawkins

although selfish in wanting to reproduce (and hence have spawned complex structures of tissue and forms of intelligence over the millions of years that they have been evolving, in order to protect and enhance their ability to play the reproduction game), they have not evolved into structures that are selfish in the classic 'survival of the fittest' type, as many people erroneously think. Whilst selfishness may be a useful trait, so is altruism and the ability to cooperate, among others. The 'fittest' refers to those who utilise the best traits in the most successful way, not some tooth and claw idealism (although it might manifest this way in many species).

As a result, and as societies of these individuals (made up of selfish genes) have grown more complex, we see that all types of persons can thrive in society. But moreover, in a social society fully selfish individuals will not often be reproductively successful. Reproduction is about carrying genes on, and our natural desire to protect our own genes is in competition with our natural desires to protect our children and parents (who share on average 50% of our genes), our brothers and sisters (who also share around 50%), and perhaps more relevantly we have developed – at times long before we could be called humans – a social desire to protect others as a mutual matter of developing both a society and fulfilling social relationships in which ourselves, our young and our relatives are looked after with minimised risk of them being destroyed.

Dawkins himself is not at pains to explain the selfish or sociopathic behaviour which society still suffers. It becomes apparent that in any society where people are kind to one another outside of family bonds, this will leave opportunity for a few 'users' to take advantage of kindness and to flourish without returning any kindness back into society. But in several species, we see 'users' to be rare. Dawkins highlights the examples of vampire bats, from the work of G.S Wilkinson,[29] to show why this might be.

Vampire bats feed at night and they don't often get lucky with it, but when they do hit a feed they tend to get a big one. As a result, Wilkinson saw many cases of altruism whereby bats would feed others who hadn't gotten a feed from the night (the majority were kin: at least 77 out of 110 cases). This is a pay-off that appears to occur in nature in several species, and is an evolutionarily successful one. And when tested under controlled conditions, the bats themselves would withhold feed from starving bats in other groups who were not known to be 'givers' previously. In other words, if there is a risk you are a 'user', you are much less likely to get help in your hour of need. Hence 'users' do not do well.

In a society as developed as human civilisation, with social stigma and legal punishments resulting in 'users' getting a reputation and most likely comeuppance (a system well beyond the complexity of any bat societies), it isn't a great strategy to be selfish in your dealings with others. Similarly, one might claim that the biggest benefit to us all is a rational understanding of altruism as a universal concept (this is something I will discuss throughout by discussing the rationality of morality as a purely selfish matter, though it is certainly not what I am advocating). If it makes evolutionary sense for many other species to develop altruistic tendencies in more basic social scenarios, we can multiply this need a great deal to recognise how important it is in consciously monitored, complex civilisations like that of human beings. We can also show that given our rational abilities, we can consciously understand

---

[29] TSG p 231. Original source is Wilkinson, G. S. (1984) Reciprocal food-sharing in the vampire bat. *Nature* 308, 181-4.

the need to not be 'users' and create more effective flourishing for everyone. At least in theory.

As Dawkins brings this research together, one thing becomes obvious. Morality is not a trait that evolved solely in human beings. Altruism is a trait present in a variety of other species, and this shows it plays a vital role in the game of gene reproduction. Morality at its most basic point is a development of wanting to protect our genes, like the more basic kind of morality in the vampire bats, rather than referring to a development of 'intuitions' with which to identify separate, independent moral facts existing in the universe. This is not to say certain *objective* moral facts cannot exist (as I will examine later), but independent moral facts like this certainly are the stuff of fantasy, as is the idea that selfishness is some desirable, natural characteristic that is 'rational' and optimal to hold.

Relative and Objective Ethics

This basic understanding of how morality evolved, and why, is vital to forming a moral theory. The theory that initially seems to be best placed in taking it on board is moral relativism. The most rational current form of which is the idea that morality as we conceive it doesn't exist, is a social construct, and thus should be deemed relative. Many of us hold some sort of belief in this. There are no independent moral facts hiding under rocks or in trees, and our intuitions about morality are simply tools for social success, instilled in us by millions of years of evolution. Morality is the stuff of opinions. So there should be no need to hold people to moral laws that do not really exist. It often manifests as cultural relativism, which notes that if a code of morality exists in any culture then we should respect that as having its own truth values within that culture. Morality in any given culture is a socially useful tool, and we should just follow moral laws and codes wherever they take us, dependent on which culture we're in.

To some degree the moral relativists have a point. They are right to say independent moral facts do not exist, and that morality evolved as a useful thing to have in society. But this is where the opinions of people like the neuroscientist and philosopher Sam Harris come into play. In *The Moral Landscape* Harris intends to debunk the idea that science and rationality have nothing to say about morality, and along with showing religious and spiritual ideas about morality to be invalid he also has to counter the relativist idea that there are no facts to be found in morality[30] which so many scientists tend to believe. Harris sees conscious creatures as the subjects morality refers to, and his further claim is that the concept of 'well-being' captures all that we can intelligibly value morally. 'Morality' – whatever people's associations with this term happen to be – really relates to the intentions and behaviours that affect the well-being of conscious creatures.[31]

Harris is not blind to the ideas of evolution[32] and the social development of morality that moral relativism is built on. What Harris goes on to state with his theory of morality as the well-being of conscious creatures, is that it doesn't matter how it evolved, those things that are known to be worse for the well-being of conscious creatures are immoral. This makes sense with what we know morality to be in society,

---

[30] *The Moral Landscape*, Sam Harris
[31] ibid, page 32-33.
[32] Harris is the founder of Project Reason, one of the popularly known 'Four Horseman of the anti-apocalypse' and writes variously about the problems with religion and non-scientific accounts of 'creation'. He's a strong voice for evolution.

and quite possibly counters the individually liberalist ideal of assigning morality a 'relativist status' to be respected regardless of what it entails. But his ideas are open to all number of problems before they can do this. Relativism is an intuitive idea once we understand the evolutionary role of morality, so are Harris' ideas defensible? I will examine what are, in my mind at least, the two main criticisms of Harris' ideas.

Moral realism

Harris states his support of moral realism loud and clear: "While moral realism and consequentialism have both come under pressure in philosophical circles, they have the virtue of corresponding to many of our intuitions about how the world works."[33] He goes on to state his agreement with consequentialism,[34] noting it to be the underpinning of most moral theory (including religion, which he is fiercely critical of). He also talks of how it doesn't make sense to speak of morality in any way without ascribing moral realism in the sense of consequentialism. Yet at any point does Harris get over the problems with classic moral realism? For those non-philosophers, moral realism is the idea that moral facts exist and can be discovered.

---

[33] TML, page 62.

[34] Consequentialism is defined by the Stanford Encyclopedia of Philosophy as "the view that normative properties depend only on consequences." What Harris means, in layman terms, is that there could be no moral fact which entailed worse overall consequences for sentient individuals – as ethics is about their well-being. On Harris' view, morality is about consequences and not just principles. A minority of moral views state that it is principles and not consequences which we should be interested in, and understandably this appears to be dying out – as Harris states, even religions at some point are consequentialist, by judging the perceived spiritual consequences of an action to be what we should be interested in.

I don't believe he does. Harris still appears to be trapped within the problem of admitting that he is just assuming that the moral fact relating to 'well-being' exists. Will we find this moral fact while studying the ground under rocks? No. Will we be able to imply its existence when examining the issue like with the laws of quantum mechanics? No. In fact the only thing backing up our intuitions that these moral facts simply exist independently is just that: our intuitions. The idea that morality simply *is* defined as well-being, and thus is righteous, because we say so. Because we intuitively believe it. And we can hardly take the same position Harris does on the absurdity of religion (that it's only supported by culturally ingrained intuitions) if we don't extend that to the absurdity of any made up but desired facts, like those he identifies in morality. If such ideas don't appear to exist, we should be honest in admitting it.

'Is' implies 'ought'

The other issue Harris faces, and like so many others fails to answer fully, comes in the form of the 'is-ought problem'. Harris' argument is essentially that it makes no sense to talk of morality as anything else but to do with maximising the 'well-being' of conscious creatures. And as such there isn't any reason why science cannot develop a branch of morality to do this, by examining the effects of behaviours and activities, and deeming them immoral based on their effect as concluded by scientific investigation.

There is much to be said of Harris' attempt, especially the latter part of noting that just because science may not be able to judge an activity as immoral now, does not mean science doesn't work as a theory of morality. There are many things science doesn't know, but it doesn't mean we should abandon it in favour of accepting hearsay or spiritual justifications for truth instead, as I argued earlier. However, the answer he provides to the is-ought problem does not fall into the positive aspects of the theory.

The problem itself can be explained quite simply: just because Harris correctly identifies *how* morality is currently defined, it doesn't mean that morality *should* therefore be taken as factual. Indeed, Harris himself admits there are plenty of things we currently allow for which are immoral (the case in point being religious dogmatism). Proof, if proof were needed, that the status of things doesn't imply their justification.

If someone were to successfully create a defensible theory of morality, able to marry itself with scientific reality, then both of these issues would need to be addressed before it could be taken seriously: that 'is' doesn't imply 'ought' and that moral facts don't seem to naturally exist. I believe Harris' attempt is one of the better that we currently have, and yet these two criticisms stop it from even being considered. We are currently a long way from a rational morality at this stage.

Rational. Irrational. Non-Rational. The problem in a nutshell

A rationalist friend of mine argues (and summarises the position very nicely) that we must draw a clear difference between what is rational and what is irrational, but also what is non-rational. Things like religion, or other 'woo' ideas like karmic energy or psychic powers that are disproved by rational examination, are irrational notions which should not form part of understood facts or scientific knowledge. The argument goes that we must draw a difference between irrational ideas, and things like morality which are not *irrational* but *non-rational*.

This is a distinction many academics seem keen to make, many rationally inclined moral theorists would agree with, and is one that moral realism seems to be heavily based on. Yet, there is no reason to draw a distinction between the irrational and the non-rational at all. We can't be sure independent moral facts exist to the same degree that we can't be sure God exists. Indeed, if we were to survey people as to their base reason why it is necessary to act morally, one may find that there are as many people (if not more) who act morally from fear of divine punishment as from belief in 'non-rational' moral facts. This wouldn't be important, of course, as we know that people can delude themselves en masse. Entire societies can be based on irrational beliefs, and entire moral codes can be formed around persuasive delusions. So the fact that so many people believe in independent moral facts does nothing to allay the obvious problems with them.

The problem for rational moral realists, though, is in answering the question of why exactly moral facts are non-rational, whilst things like religious facts are irrational. We know that in every other area of truth, no matter how abstract our facts get, we can link them back to direct and provable observations of reality: evidence. With morality there is only one link back to reality – the link back to our intuitions. Moral realism essentially believes that it is our intuitions that are pointing to moral facts. Yet religious theorists say the same thing. Anyone can claim just about anything is 'non-rational', and indeed many spiritualist profiteers do. If we began indulging this idea of the non-rational into other areas of life, we'd soon find it problematic; vaccinations wouldn't have to pass tests, or in Britain we could cut our spending on the National Health Service by claiming that non-rational facts show that fewer people will become ill this year. Non-rational facts shown by the prime minister's intuitions about how well their policies are going, perhaps.

There is no reason to differentiate between the irrational and the non-rational, and as far as we can see the distinction is drawn only because there is currently no understood way to ground morality in science. We want it to not be *irrational*, so we call it *non-rational*. This is a problem. If all we have are our intuitions, and therefore we have to make assumptions about the truth-values of our intuitions like we don't with science, then there is no reason to consider morality objective. In essence, if all we have is the non-rational, then all we have is the irrational, and the moral relativists are partly correct that there are no objective truths about morality (though, as I will examine shortly, they are also irrational, but in a wholly separate way). Yet I believe there is a way in which we can justify viewing morality as objective.

Chapter 2: A Rational Solution

What should be intuitive by this point, and indeed what society is rapidly beginning to think, is that morality isn't grounded in a factual, provable way like many moral philosophers might have us believe. There are no moral facts hiding under rocks, or being implied by the study of circles, etc. Indeed, the study of the evolution of morality implies there is no need for such concepts to explain human behaviour. With relation to rational analysis, current moral theory is shown to be wanting. I am not the first person to notice this weakness in moral philosophy; the philosopher John Mackie (in particular) had written arguments very similar to those in the last chapter before I was even born.[35] Presumably, his, and many other similar arguments, stay largely in the dark among moral philosophers for fear of what they might logically entail. The remaining issue is exactly on that subject: can we reliably show morality to objectively exist at all?

Before I argue that we can, let's make note that a rational theory of morality must take into account three important points.

a) Science is a fine way of determining truth. We need to be able to provide evidence and rationale in order to attribute facts. If morality is to be factual, it needs to be scientifically viable in the same way that other science is.

---

[35] *Ethics: Inventing Right and Wrong.* J. L. Mackie. 1977. Mackie believed, as the title of his book suggests, that we need to invent ethics as they do not exist independently.

b) Morality cannot exist upon fantastical notions of independent moral truths. These are unscientific.

c) The state of morality as it is, or more succinctly of well-being as the current marker of morality, does not by itself provide justification for morality to continue as it is.

If nothing else, what I have done so far is provide support for these ideas and it's from here that I'll attempt to formulate a solution to the problem of marrying reality with morality. Please, before reading further, assume this blank slate case of morality as stated above. Try to drop any preconceptions and personal beliefs about God, moral facts formed by intuition, etc. Try to drop everything except the facts: that morality evolved as a social matter, that altruism is useful in a developed society, and that morality doesn't appear to exist outside societies of sentient individuals. It's from here that I hope a theory of morality can be rationally invoked.

Is 'ought' the right way to think about morality?

We saw in the first chapter that an 'is' doesn't justify an 'ought'; the way things are does not tell us how they should be. Harris falls foul of this, and yet one of the positive aspects of his theory is that he states ought is a relatively unimportant term compared to the status it receives in moral theory. Perhaps he has a point. We live in a world where we can be scientifically assured that free will is largely mythical, as determinism shows us how at no point are our actions the cause of a personal spirit or soul, but rather are the effect of our genes and our experiences;

none of which can be traced to any sort of 'fault' on our part.[36] We didn't choose our genes, and we didn't choose the initial experiences which led our lives to where we are today (see chapter 7 for a fuller description of determinism and free will). At no point could we realistically have chosen otherwise, given who we were at those times. As such, the notion of ought seems a little misguided, and as Harris states, "This notion of ought is an artificial and needlessly confusing way to think about moral choice."[37] To a degree, Harris is right. We are not responsible for our actions in a strict 'we could have chosen otherwise' respect, so we must take notions of ought not in their classic sense of defining what is worthy of blame and praise, but merely as a guide to our behaviour. We still, however, need a justification for ought statements in order to describe aspects of rightness and wrongness. Rightness and wrongness refer to things we ought to do or not do, so the connection is a necessary one; without them, morality is meaningless. One can disagree with the historical or classic philosophical sense of the word, but one can't disagree with the fundamentally necessary concept. For morality to be anything other than relative, ought rules must be formulated – morality is all about 'oughts' and 'ought nots', and without justifying their use we have no reason to imply morality exists. 'Oughts' cannot be assumed for the same reason that gods or Supermen cannot.

---

[36] Many still argue that scientifically supported ideas like determinism are compatible with us having free will. However there is no proof that this is the case. There is as much evidence that rocks have free will as humans do. We are simply highly evolved apes, and there's nothing special about us that takes us out-with the basic scientific discovery of cause and effect. If you are still in doubt with regards to how free will does not exist, please suspend disbelief until chapter 7 where the subject is discussed more fully.

[37] TML p 38

Harris lets us further into his insight as to what morality really is with his next comments: "We must build our better selves into our laws, tax codes, and institutions. Knowing that we are generally incapable of valuing two children more than either child alone, we must build a structure that reflects and enforces our deeper understanding of human well-being."[38] Here Harris is making the point that we perhaps do not intuitively know what is right (and in marketing campaigns we are shown to irrationally give more concern to the suffering of one individual child than to two[39]) but of more relevance is that he shows how the essence of morality is not so much about discovering what we ought to do, so much as figuring out what we could all do to increase the well-being of conscious creatures. He doesn't say why one should care about conscious creatures other than oneself in the first place though, and so still falls foul of the is-ought problem despite trying to redefine it.

In part, of course, Harris is right to claim classic notions of ought are flawed. But that isn't to say we don't need an 'ought' to guide behaviour; one that morality could therefore be drawn from, and one that could be factually identified. All Harris still appears to be doing is drawing an ought from an is. No matter how greatly we criticise the classic conceptions of ought, this is still logically invalid. Yes, we do define morality as being about the well-being of sentient individuals, but why *ought* we care about morality in the first place? We can't very well discard the idea of religion, fairies and karma as unscientific if we are clinging to morality on the very same assertion that we simply want

---

[38] TML p 70
[39] Harris references Slovic, P. (2007). "If I look at the mass I will never act": Psychic numbing and genocide. *Judgement and Decision Making*, 2(2), 79-95.

to pretend it's real. Morality needs a scientific backing. Harris appears to be knocking on the right doors, but not quite opening them.

Finding an ought

Finding an 'ought' from an 'is' has perplexed philosophers for centuries, most famously noted in the work of David Hume in the 18th century. We can be assured that we can't derive any justifiable ought from any naturally existing fact about the world. The two are incompatible.

However, human society has gone well beyond 'naturally existing' situations. Thus, quite simply, we solve the is-ought problem in a justifiable manner if we can identify a societal situation in which an ought can be logically derived. So, if we were all to agree that we want there to be a moral code, and we can all agree upon a rough definition of morality (such as 'morality is about maximising the well-being of sentient individuals'), then we can use these 'is' facts to formulate moral 'ought' facts. This is the only way around the is-ought problem, as we have created a situation in which an ought (moral code) can be derived from an is (agreement that we all want a form of moral code). A collective, foundational agreement allows for a collective, objective form of morality.

Still, the idea of 'inventing' a moral code like this has many more nuances in order to become rational and not merely arbitrary; we have solved the is-ought problem, but that is all so far. If we want there to exist a form of morality which is objective and which can be studied as such, then we need to take steps towards agreement, which can be summarised as follows:

Majority societal agreement that we want there to be an objective theory of morality in the first place. Either we want to disagree with ideas like murder, rape and other acts we view as heinous, or we don't. If we want to cast such ideas as fundamentally immoral, then we need to agree that objective morality should be something which we 'invent', formulate and then stick by (building it into law and wider society).

Once agreed, we have to work with our best definition of what morality actually is, as the foundation to extend moral laws from. Harris has provided us with an idea that it is about the well-being of sentient individuals. Whilst such a definition will always be open to advancement, it makes sense to stick with fair, rational conceptions. I'll argue throughout the book what I believe to be the core areas/ideas inherent in a rational theory of morality, but Harris does seem to have hit home with his initial definition.

Once defined and agreed, the subject should be handed over to science. Science is the best method that we have of determining truth and rationally extending ideas, whilst also our best method of eliminating bias, unfairness and cheating. If morality is to be viewed as truly objective, and we've already agreed that we want it to be so, then it simply has to become a science in which answers are based on and answerable to evidence rather than opinion. Not taking this important final step means we are answering the is-ought problem without taking morality onto its logical conclusions, which seems self-defeating when the goal was a more rational form of morality.

A guiding 'ought' principle?

By following the steps above, we can carve a rational theory of morality which is objective and not relative. The last step – handing morality over to science – is the most important part, as it means morality has to at least comply with the rules of science and not be arbitrarily extended. But in order to do this, moral science can only make one basic assumption, just as other science can: that we *ought to be rational*. In other words, we set the foundational principle that morality is about maximising the well-being of sentient individuals, and then we devote ourselves to being rational, and only rational, about extending it.

This assumption of rationality is at the bottom of every science: we have to be as rational as we can, testing experience and anecdote to develop ideas and truths which we can replicate and explain. If we develop a theory of morality with only one guiding rule - that we ought to be rational – there seems no reason why we can't have an objective, scientific theory of morality. We follow the three steps mentioned previously to create a science of morality, and then we retain a guiding principle that we ought to be rational.

This kind of rational 'ought' principle is also not so much an assumption to make regarding morality, so much as an assumption we implicitly make regarding everything. Science is based on it, our minds work in a way which strives for it (indeed, beliefs can't stick with anyone without them believing the belief, which is a rational system. People don't believe things in spite of believing them, which would be truly irrational). We ought to be rational if we want the truth – something science has known since its primitive foundations. And just as rationality shows classic theories of morality to be lacking, it shows that rationality is the only assumption morality can make if it wants to be scientific. And, once again, not submitting the theory to rationality is self-defeating, if the idea was to create a justifiable and rational theory of morality.

Why does a rational morality need to be objective, or science-based?

A clear objection will be to ask why I think this three-step idea of creating moral science is any more truthful or scientific than a relativist form of morality. This is an important question, as the answer hits right on the issue of why moral science (as a consensually, societally agreed type) is desperately necessary. Relativist logic assumes that because morality is a certain way (i.e., it evolved relatively) we should thus view it that way. That's only true in one sense: we should not ignore facts about the evolution of morality by stating, like spiritual accounts of morality do, that moral facts exist in our intuitions or our hearts. However, science certainly does not say that we *should* do that which science tells us we can. Richard Dawkins suffered this kind of uninformed criticism with his publishing of *The Selfish Gene* in 1976. He was the subject of many liberal accusations that he was justifying selfish, conservative politics by stating that we consist of 'selfish' genes. The criticism failed to notice that just because scientific fact tells us we are a certain way, or in this case that our genes are a certain way, does not mean that we *ought* to act that way.

And this is where a theory of rational morality becomes necessary. Relativism can account perfectly well for why morality exists, but it is not rational unless one ignores the is-ought problem. Morality did evolve as a relative, social tool, but that is no logical reason to suppose that we should observe it in the future as such.

So we are rationally justified in going above relativism, and creating something objective. But in order for it to be truly objective, it also needs to be part of a collective method that strives for objectivity - the

34

only human method that does this in any meaningful way is organised science. Once, as described in the first two steps, we have a foundation for a theory (a societally agreed one) we simply need to throw the one scientific assumption in: that we ought to be rational. We then have an incredibly useful blueprint, and also an incredibly simple one, of determining moral facts based upon a set moral principle (that we ought to be rational) in relation to a foundational definition which we are being rational about. Just like physics asks us to be rational about our observations in physics experiments, moral science asks us to be rational in bringing about greater well-being for sentient individuals in moral experiments (which occur daily in our lives) due to this being a basic moral principle which we all agree with.

A different type of science: approaching the nuances of the theory

There's no doubt that the types of facts we are dealing with in morality are fundamentally different – facts in physics are true whether you believe them or not, or whether humans exist or not, whereas moral facts are more socially grounded. They are relative to our species, perhaps, and could theoretically change based on justified value changes. This is not relativity in the way moral relativism suggests, e.g. that morality is just what exists to guide the society. Entire cultures could still be less developed than others in moral terms (by explicitly creating less well-being for sentient individuals), in the same way that entire cultures can be less developed in health-care terms.

More accurately, the relativity aspect of scientific morality relates to changes of a more elementary level, i.e. if as organisms we began pursuing pain rather than pleasure, the moral facts would look a great deal different to how they look now, as we pursue pleasure and want to avoid pain. The facts of morality are entirely dependent on certain fundamental factors, as fundamental factors determine what well-being consists of.[40] In this sense, and this sense only, moral science is relative. The same is not true of physical science, where facts exist objectively.

We also can't make the same claims about independent moral facts and physics facts: the claim that 'killing is wrong' is not of the same truth value as 'gravity is the force that pulls us to Earth'. Strong evidence would be needed to disprove either, but we can imagine situational evidence where the first statement is shown to be incorrect (i.e. killing in self-defence, or where the choice is between two deaths), whereas evidence to disprove the latter is not currently plausible. But this difference in status also doesn't mean we should claim moral truths are simply relative. Sure, there are some elements of relativity to science (let's remember that a perfectly straight line on Earth is curved when viewed from space, and understanding this type of relativity of perspective is important), but we don't claim it is relative depending on the society that invented it. Physics exists because it is useful, and morality exists because it is useful. They still each have objective truths, as I will argue they must.

But if we can choose to create a scientific theory of morality, can't we choose to create a scientific theory of anything?

---

[40] This is certainly an area for further study, in order to flesh out a more universal idea of what this kind of morality entails, and how we decide which values are important and deserving of different rules, or which are simply cultural errors. However, in this book I will stick to the simpler topic of moral theory in this world, with human beings of the type who currently exist.

Morality is different from other science (admittedly) in the respect that we would be choosing to make it science, in a way that we don't have to do with physical science. With physics or biology, for example, we are observing phenomena and studying them, thus discovering truths about the physical world which we can subject to tests and evidence. Whereas with morality we are deciding it to be rational, based on an agreed need and foundation, and then subjecting the whole concept to scientific and rational discourse. So the criticism might ask 'If we can choose to make morality a science, why can't we choose to make anything else a science?' A science of homeopathy, perhaps?

This is a valid concern. But, primarily, we mustn't confuse our labelling it as 'moral science' with it being a natural science. It isn't. We could call it anything, it makes little difference. I use the term science only because we should treat its investigations and extensions like we treat those in science; calling it science helps to define that we need a similarly strong methodology to that of the scientific method in order to gain results.

A more difficult question would be 'Why is it okay to do it with morality and not with homeopathy?' There are obvious reasons of pragmatism, but I think there are more serious concerns. Homeopathy is a form of alternative 'medical' treatment whereby, depending on the illness, a patient will receive a water solution with an impossibly small amount of a certain active ingredient dissolved in it as a cure. In scientific tests, homeopathy is shown to work no better than a placebo (placebos are scientifically much more interesting than fake cures like homeopathic treatments provide, but that's another story[41]) and there's good reason for that; the amount of active ingredient in homeopathic treatments is so small that we are talking a ratio of less than one drop in the entirety of the world's oceans. These treatments are placebos, scientifically speaking, but the practitioners activate the placebo effect especially well by giving the patients time, care and a garble of pseudo-science regarding the treatment itself. This is the placebo effect done in the most deceptive, but intelligent of ways. Unsurprisingly, many in the scientific community are up in arms regarding this treatment and the problems it causes for the understanding of science in society, not to mention the irrational nature of governments spending millions on these 'cures' which can be shown to not work.

So why can't we choose to make homeopathy a science? Firstly, ideas like homeopathy can't be subjected to scientific methodology at any point; trials show it doesn't work, so even if we assumed it did, how could we study extensions in it scientifically, when no homeopathic solution has effects different to any other? A scientific acceptance of homeopathy could only actually go so far as to say that each homeopathic treatment works due to the placebo effect, and thus all are equally effective. And science already says that; it's not a science of homeopathy,

---

[41] We need turn no further than the first resource linked, *Bad Science*, for yet further explanation on this (the book reads like an introductory course in scientific method for those of us who are not scientists by trade). Placebos have been found to be effective on a sliding scale, whereby the more dramatic an intervention, the more effective the placebo is at curing the ailment. For instance, one sugar pill is more effective than two sugar pills, an injection is more effective still, and even more dramatic interventions like perceived surgery can claim to have even better results, when in all three cases nothing medicinal is actually done. These are not anecdotally posited ideas, they are scientifically supported and they reveal a great deal about the way to view illness.

it's a science of placebos. The foundations for homeopathy are decidedly more shaky than those of morality.

If we were to be honest and scientific about homeopathy, we couldn't back it in the way we can back rational morality. We can't have a scientific theory of homeopathy for the same reason we can't have a scientific theory of fairies; it doesn't make sense, even if we invent it, because the outcomes are bogus, as are the scientific foundations. If we could show that homeopathy was good for human well-being, with few if any negative effects, then we would have an argument for justifying it (though not for making it a science, as society agreeing to make a type of placebo a science – like we have to with morality – would ruin the effects of the placebo). However, there are huge moral problems with it anyway. I will not delve into details here, but is it safe to be confusing people with scientific sounding ideas which are really bunk, but telling them it's science? Especially in a society where so many distrust science and fail to understand it? Similarly, how safe is it to ask people to throw their faith behind a cure that doesn't work – even if the placebo effect accompanying it cures this small medical issue - and risk them refusing genuine medical treatment in the future due to this reliance and faith in pseudo-science? And finally, is it really good for people to be of the type that they throw their support behind things that they don't understand, based on the acceptance of authority? Sure we need authority figures often, but with science and technology people could delve into the reasons why these things work if they really want to (or at least grasp them slightly), whereas homeopathy asks them to suspend their rational abilities and instincts in favour of full-blown faith. All of these issues, among others, would need solving before we even considered homeopathy a useful treatment, let alone consider debauching the tried and tested method of science by intentionally deceiving entire societies with 'a science of homeopathy'. Add to that the fact that it's literally impossible to create a science out of something with non-causal outcomes (each treatment is the same level of placebo, and will cure no illness better than any other) and we justify why we haven't created a science of homeopathy.

A more difficult criticism of rational morality might be found in picking a more rationally able topic: 'Why can't we create a scientific theory of playing basketball?' Well, we can! There's an awful lot of science used in basketball, and if there is public need to create one then we should begin institutionalising it.

I firmly believe there is more need for a science of morality, as I believe it's more important to deal with death, suffering and well-being than with playing a sport better or more effectively than someone else, but this is just my opinion and thus is open to analysis. There is no reason why there couldn't be a science of basketball though, and some sports scientists exist exactly for these reasons. What do you think coaches of basketball teams do, for example? They try to objectively find ways to be better than their opponents, which will reflect in the victory within the rules of the game. This is, in a very real sense, an amateur attempt at basketball science. Each have their favoured theories and ideas, they simply don't regularly make them too scientific, as they trust their gut feelings or emotional reactions instead.

An even more challenging criticism would be one that picked a subject with conceptually exact similarity to morality: 'If we can create a scientific theory of morality, why can't we create a scientific theory of what are objectively the best colours?' This one is more difficult to answer, but essentially is a mix between the basketball and homeopathy versions of the question. Like with basketball, I am open to admitting 'we can' if we find reason for creating a 'science of the best colours', but then what evidence are you going to use? There doesn't seem to be any basis, like there is for morality. We know about the uses of colours, the psychological effects, or the physical make-up of the light, but we don't know anything about why one colour would be 'better' than another, or what 'better' would even be referring to when it comes to colours as a universal concept. Whereas morality is important to human civilisation, being a rationally evolved and necessary concept, favourite colours appear to be only a personal preference, with most people harbouring no strong feelings at all.

My feelings on why morality differs from colours are down to the importance to civilisation. I mean, perhaps within human society one can decipher reasons for judging a person's favourite colour wrong, based on the rational nature of having a favourite colour. I can't, but one day someone might be able to. At this stage, I can't envision such a science needing to come to the foreground, as I can't imagine on what grounds majority societal opinion will have cause or reason for agreeing that such a science is necessary. Raising a similarity between favourite colours and morality is conceptually acceptable (both are abstract ideas which we would need to explicitly make into science) but historically and referentially ridiculous. But if disagreement about colours meant our entire civilisation was stagnating, powerless to overcome the problems of long since debunked conservative economic theory, then we'd be in a position to perhaps consider such a thing.

So why *can* we decide to make morality rational? The answer is a split between the ability for extending outcomes rationally (which differentiates it from the science of homeopathy), and civilizational importance (which differentiates it from basketball and colours). If we consensually agree that morality is important, and it needs to be neutral (and by definition morality does need to be neutral and fair, as that's what morality is – hence why I keep making the point that there is no reason to theorise morality logically if we aren't going to follow through on what that entails), then logic is begging us to do two things:

Admit that none of us implicitly have sacred knowledge about morality which we can pass onto each other; there are no 'moral facts' that exist independent of human culture for us to learn.

Create a socially constructed science of morality instead. Sociology also doesn't exist out with human culture, and yet we have a whole area of academia studying and making progress in it. It split from subjects like philosophy, and thrives on scientific method. There is no reason why morality can't do this too.

In a nutshell, this brief piece of reasoning on 'why morality, but not...' should soothe many of the critically important issues with an idea like rational morality. How it leaves philosophers feeling (morality being one of the last real forms of truth finding which is granted to philosophy over science) is another matter, for another book. There is no doubt, though, that morality should be a science when we look at it rationally.

Why ought we be rational?

The fact that we ought to be rational is one already accepted by all forms of scientific investigation and is the one form of experiment and truth which is already respected by everyone in society. It is the one basic assumption all scientific endeavours make, and that all people value no matter how much they claim not to: they wouldn't be doing *anything* without it.[42] As long as a moral theory doesn't make any assumptions other than that we ought to be rational, then it is scientifically viable.

If we doubt that we ought to be rational, in order to find what is right or what is true, then we are creating a paradox for ourselves. Every word we speak and every idea we formulate owes itself, at some point, to rationality. Doubting that we ought to be rational misses not just *the* point, but *every* point. Every criticism of this principle itself implies the rationality that it aims to delete (by virtue of the nature of criticisms, which aim to be a rational criticism that holds intellectual water). Rationality is the study of reality. It is the observation and development of our understanding about the world as it is. We therefore ought to be rational, and as objective as possible about it, if we want to discover facts about something. Doubting this is almost unintelligible. It is not a societally agreed moral ought that makes the propositions true, but rather it is a logical necessity for truth finding; if one isn't being rational in their endeavours, then one isn't doing any more than finding subjective truth. Positing an 'ought to be rational' when truth finding is like positing an 'ought to be truth finding'. It's a logical and intimately bound necessity.

---

[42] A person will always act rationally in some basic sense. No matter how spiritually inclined, or seeing ghosts around them, they are always making decisions as conscious subjects of a life. It is impossible for human beings to decide to do things 'randomly', and were we to have a perfect understanding of human behaviour and every effect on a person's mind, we would in fact be able to predict a person's next thought, action or decision. We might never genuinely have these kinds of technological capabilities, just like we may never have perfect capabilities for predicting the behaviour for other primates, but this doesn't mean our actions could ever be irrational as a systematic matter.

43

Rationality is as close to an ought as one can get in moral theory, and the ought involved is one of a profoundly different type to the ought that one might claim to exist 'to be compassionate' or 'to be kind' in current theories of ethics. Claiming we ought to do anything *but* be rational is to make an assumption that one can't justify (which is unfortunately something that moral philosophers have a rich history of). Claiming we ought to be rational, however, is perfectly justifiable if we want to engage in any form of discussion about morality in the first place. As mentioned previously, it is a logical necessity. Kindness or compassion might be rational responses in certain situations (and so might be derived as 'ought rules' from the principle of rationality in certain situations), but they aren't provable, or anything more than personally preferable principles at the outset. Whereas an obligation to be rational is necessary before we even start to communicate an idea. As assumptions go, rationality is the basis of everything: a self-proving assumption that one can rely on.

Is rationality the basic principle of science?

Many would criticise this by claiming that science makes several assumptions, not just that of rationality. This argument takes a couple of different paths in modern conversations. One is the argument that scientists make inherent assumptions in order to prove experiments: assumptions such as 'phenomena can be understood', or 'physical laws are the same everywhere'. But even if a scientist is throwing their faith behind these extra assumptions (we could call them 'second order assumptions'), they are still either open to change (given new evidence) or else backed by the deeper assumption that we ought to be rational. The latter is often the case, as these second order assumptions are tested and shown to be evident time and time again, so the rational principle can take them as true until proven otherwise. It is rational for them to make these assumptions based on this justified reasoning.

The other form of the argument is that scientists must explicitly assume things about the validity of their observations, or validity of observation as a method at all. The claim here seems slightly deeper than the previous one, in claiming to show that science has more than one first order assumption. But again, any assumption like those claimed here is tested and subjected to evidence also. The truth is that there may be an awful lot of ideas which scientists learn, and thus take for granted (assume) when doing science, but that is because science in general works. They have no need to test each assumption in every experiment (whether it be about the validity of their observations, or the nature of physical laws) as both the historical experience of other scientists, as well as things like observations demonstrably working and not returning unexpected error, already examines and tests those assumptions implicitly. Even when these assumptions are undermined, they are changed, so this shows the assumption was not fundamental in the first place. The assumption about the validity of our observations, for example, is tested, amended and sometimes even dropped in areas where we can't directly observe the phenomena or are prone to mistakes in observation (scientific experiments in dark rooms, perhaps, or even some erring results in quantum mechanics).

In situations where second order assumptions are changed it is that single first order assumption (the principle of rationality) that changes them. There are many famous examples of these second order assumptions changing throughout history: the switching from an assumption about Earth being at the centre of the solar system, scientists increasing the number of known elements, and perhaps most famously the discovery of certain unintuitive events at particle level. These changes in turn demonstrate further evidence in favour of science accepting rationality implicitly, and also evidence that these other second order assumptions are not assumptions of science but rather are part of the body of knowledge which science consists of (which is discovered and developed, rather than assumed). The only constant that has remained is the guiding principle that we ought to be rational.

We might say that within individual experiments a scientist is assuming the usefulness of repetition, or the validity of isolating variables, or perhaps even the advantages of thoroughly noting the method. As a matter of explicit assumptions within individual tests, it is fair to say that scientists are assuming a great deal. But each of these assumptions is backed by every piece of scientific investigation that takes place, and so as a fundamental matter of the nature and philosophy of science, it is true that the only basic assumption that science makes is regarding rationality. And in truth, even rationality is only assumed because each and every methodologically successful experiment (whether the results were successful or not) or scientific advancement justifies this single assumption. Science is a strong method of truth finding, whilst rationality is, for good reason, its only foundational principle.

Can we disprove rationality as a principle by arguing against it irrationally?

It is here that we reach one of the more bizarre forms of rational-focused criticism. Some might feel no need to accept the argument that we ought to be rational, and feel no need to formulate a rational critique of it. As if being *irrational* is a get out clause that allows one to not accept rationality as a base assumption. Again, this is still grasping at rational straws. It only makes sense to choose to be irrational as an antidote to the value of rationality, if one is already assuming that they need to make a rational argument to demonstrate incoherence or inconsistence. To do this, one must believe that rational reasoning is the opposite of incoherent or inconsistent reasoning. Yet what is that belief, if not an attempt to rationally debunk rationalism by rationally positing its opposite as true? This is a self-defeating approach.

Or, to put it simpler, if X says rationality is important and Z disagrees – thereby feeling obligated to act as irrationally as possible to prove X incorrect – then Z is trying to behave in a way which is rationally consistent with their opinion about the unimportance of rationality. This shows that rationality is so necessary for human behaviour that even the most farfetched of thought experiments still show human beings as quintessentially striving for it.

Everything, including science, needs to make one assumption to begin investigating truth. Science, as noted above, makes the strong case for that assumption being that we ought to be rational. We can't even argue this assumption without accepting it, which cements its place as a necessary and basic principle. Further assumptions above *we ought to be rational,* which allow for the irrational (like independent moral facts) violate the first assumption, and so are flawed. This is keen, logical claims making.

The state of morality as it is, or more succinctly of well-being as the current marker of morality, does not by itself provide justification for morality to continue as it is.

My claim that we ought to be rational makes no assumption that morality is a certain way and so is right. In fact, although we make all of our decisions based on some form of intention to be rational (show me someone whose brain works by not formulating decisions, and I'll admit error), most of our moral decisions could arguably be improved if we actually made the decision to extend external rational analysis and consistency to them, like we do in science.

How can an obligation to be rational lead to a decent form of morality?

It's easy to show why rationality is both an inbuilt system for human beings and a necessary one. Hence why supposing 'we ought to be rational' is a sensible scientific assumption – even in matters of moral science (a discipline which is largely invented). We stunt the growth of every form of truth finding without it. It is also relatively easy to create the conditions that allow us to draw an ought from an is. However, showing rationality to be a good way of judging morality in the real world, when it has been disregarded as such throughout history, is quite a way more difficult. In fact, prejudice against rationality as a marker of morality is rife. And yet so long as we have agreed on a definition of morality that we want and which holds up to analysis, then rationality is a perfectly acceptable tool for making moral decisions.

What it means to accept the obligation to be rational is thus to admit this, and also currently (in my opinion) Harris' entirely rational claim that morality refers only to the well-being of conscious individuals. It makes no sense for us to value trees, mountains or oceans if the well-being of conscious individuals is not at stake. Morality doesn't refer to trees, or physical facts, but rather to the well-being of individuals who can experience what happens to them. This is a rational definition of morality, as far as I can see, until we can show otherwise.

This does not mean that to be rational we simply need to accept current moral rules, like a moral relativist would, under the guise that these rules have evolved and so they work, and thus are rational. This is not so much rational as ignorant, and it falls foul of the third point which any rational theory of morality must oppose (point c: that morality being a certain way doesn't justify its continuance in this way). We must accept, perhaps, Harris' definition of morality (unless we can better it) but we don't necessarily have to accept the way things are. Take physics, for example. We find facts in physics in one society, yet if another group elsewhere shows those facts to be wrong and new ones to be correct, then those facts must change in *all* societies. Societies that are aware but don't change are wrong. A rational theory of morality must go on to accept a definition of morality, like Harris provides, to be correct until evidenced agreement can imply its incorrectness. From this base even the most culturally ingrained of acts could be scientifically shown wrong as a moral matter. Moral rules derive from rational deductions, leading from a general principle about the well-being of all conscious individuals.

But also pragmatically, to look back just 100, or even 50, years is to look back and see Western society in a worse place for women, people of colour and those in lower social classes, and so to state that where we are now is better and thereby perfectly rational and riskless, is

49

arrogant and historically ignorant. Irrational on a basic analysis, even. Indeed, speaking of the conscious species of human beings alone, the incidence of religious fundamentalist terrorism, right-wing political ignorance of non-white non-males, and a growing gap between the poorest and richest (funded by a growing category of the poorest) should tell us that this isn't the best world we could manage, and that it is still incredibly risky and irrational for all of us. It takes a fairly irrational ignorance of inequality to sum up that morality is working the best it can, even when we ignore sentient individuals other than humans (we kill and unintentionally torture 60 billion land animals alone per year).

It's rational to extend our current morality to the greatest number, and to the greatest forms of equality, and that seems to hold true as a pragmatic matter as well. Not fostering this wide-reaching equality is simply preaching for inconsistency, for moral rules that promote explicit selfishness, and this perhaps holds vicious danger for us even without considering moral science (which asks for moral code to be extended consistently, not selfishly).

Not extending this rationally created and required morality, on the basis it might benefit us or our small groups more not to extend it, is slipping into a poor form of act-utilitarianism. (And whilst I won't go into the many problems with this position immediately, it is useful to note.[43]) Indeed even the richer, better served members of society at current are still taking risks which are by no means 'rational'. We see the gap between the rich and the poor growing, and this can only be funded by a larger 'poor' group. Hence those people of power are fast diminishing their own positions of security – creating a larger group of

---

[43] This will be discussed in more detail in chapter 4.

potentially desperate and unwilling participants in social civility – simply in a vain attempt to get more money. Yet they don't need more money to improve security, and such risks are irrational (as even if protection against social crime is easily affordable, it isn't perfect) and bred from our fallible human instincts to always reach for 'more', not from some human capability to be rational (which would involve being satisfied when secure, and giving excess away to allow others to be satisfied and not dangerous to you when they struggle for survival). It is not rational to listen to the greed instinct once far-reaching security is reached.

The main thing to take away, though, is not the pragmatics. If we are to believe in and use morality, then we have to treat it like science. This means not fudging results when it suits us personally (like sacrificing another conscious individual for 'more things') by appealing to personal beliefs or intentions. A rational theory of morality, as we have so far explored, means we ought to be rational in extending rules which maximise the well-being of sentient individuals.

What's more, morality is entirely rational and has brought us to a more civilised society.[44] And civilised, productive society, as well as rational, consistent morality both demand equality and consistency. The two things almost certainly go hand in hand. The evolution of morality may have happened through self-serving interests that altruism (and

---

[44]http://www.ted.com/talks/steven_pinker_on_the_myth_of_violence.html In this talk Steven Pinker remarks that our 21st Century society produced 100 million human deaths through war and violence, however our more irrational hunter-gatherer societies (societies which are decidedly less civilised and organised) would have produced around 2 billion deaths through violence. This is a huge difference, and there is no doubt that a more civilised society, even with its questionable wars, creates less violence. Pinker's recent academic work which is referenced later in the chapter is the proof for this comment.

therefore, morality) has evolved from in the past; however, this does not mean that the rational way is to carry on viewing it in selfish terms.

Prejudice is irrational

Undoubtedly there are still unanswered objections and criticisms, which I will look across in the next chapter. For now, it would be useful to look at a couple of examples of scientific moral code in order to get some real-world ideas as to what it involves. It's important to begin adding colour to this basic sketch.

A major principle would be that prejudice is irrational. Prejudice is, morally speaking, an arbitrary deviation from rationality; the equivalent of someone claiming that gravity is actually just invisible strawberry jelly (i.e. a position obviously inconsistent with the basic rules of rationality, or misunderstanding the facts we already know about the subject). Indeed, one would have to be ignorant of the very meaning of morality or rationality to posit prejudice as consistent with it, and so the strawberry jelly is in some ways a generous analogy by gifting prejudice, as it does, with an understanding at least of the basics of moral theory. After all, someone arguing for the strawberry jelly hypothesis must at least understand that 'stickiness' is in some way a feasible explanation for 'pull'. But prejudice is the moral equivalent of bias. It is a basic scientific error that swaps consistent, useful results for random personal opinions. That's unfeasible on a basic and obvious level.

Let's also demonstrate how the pragmatic interacts with the science (in order to show that this form of morality isn't unworkable). Prejudice has a rational basis only so far as it breeds out of our fear of difference (i.e. we might push sexism, racism, xenophobia, homophobia, etc., out of a will to protect only those who look like or seem to be like us, in an effort to protect our genes).[45] It would be incredibly foolish to grant prejudice equal importance, and thereby equal standing with equality on a pragmatic level. Prejudice leads to marginalisation and violence - I don't know anyone who would claim the Western world was more civilised when racism was legally protected, or when women or people of colour could be legally owned. Indeed, there are growing academic arguments to show this point more objectively.[46]

As morality has extended, society has become a more civilised place. Of course it has. Ridding prejudice from our moral shores is an example of rationality defeating basic instinctual ideas, such as a blanket fear of outsiders. We'd welcome a conscious, mutually fulfilling, widely understood and rational morality to eliminate prejudice like this, wouldn't we? That's what would make our conscious, moral society less risky, and better for us than an instinctually, more prone to error, morality of a vampire bat society. The pragmatics seem to favour rational morality and we can't underestimate the importance of this, given that so many ignore scientific views of the world under the false assumption that it can lead to personally conceived 'immoral' actions.

---

[45] It has been suggested to me that prejudice also plays a role in protecting power, something one might come across in a Functionalist perspective of sociology. While this may be true, it is not a conscious system – there is no boardroom of people deciding that prejudice must be upheld in order to protect their power. Rather, the utilisation of prejudice in this way is incidental, and a misattribution of instincts like I discuss. It just happens to create a society where power is protected in this way.

[46] Take a look at Steven Pinker's *The Better Angels of our Nature* for instance, which charts the decline of violence throughout history, noting that there has never been a better time to be a potential victim. Pinker himself notes one of the reasons for this to be our escalating use of 'reason'.

Practical application of the rational

Earlier I mentioned one solution which many might perceive as valid, after such a discovery as rational morality like I put forth here, and that is of act-utilitarianism. This would go something like: *morality is about being rational, and thereby we don't need universal rules as much as a case-by-case analysis of the rational aspects upon every decision: that would be truly rational.* However, there are important mistakes in this thinking.

I earlier quoted Harris who states: "We must build our better selves into our laws, tax codes, and institutions. Knowing that we are generally incapable of valuing two children more than either child alone, we must build a structure that reflects and enforces our deeper understanding of human well-being." Here lies the reason why the compulsion for act-utilitarianism doesn't make sense.

A theory of rational morality, as I am explaining it, does appeal to the desire to be rational, and to the basic assumption that we ought to be rational. However, this does not mean that we will suddenly become rational machines ourselves, able to foresee the future and calculate all the possible outcomes in any given situation. As also mentioned earlier, we are evolutionarily disposed to erroneous decisions about morality (such as taking on board the negative experience of one child, and giving it more attention than the experience of two, or perhaps even a million children). Fighting those errors which are hardwired into our make-up almost certainly means that we need laws and rules, and rational extensions of those as a general matter.

Undoubtedly this will mean that some things are forbidden that should be allowed, or in some cases our hands might be legally tied for doing the right thing. Clumsy but well-intentioned rules, we might call these. Consider, for example, the laws regarding human murder. One might wish they were changed to allow for euthanasia but recognise that doing so would allow the law to be left open for all manner of irresponsible acts by questionable individuals. My theory of morality states we ought to be rational, but I do not for a second foresee a day when no one acts irrationally as a moral matter. Like with any science, we cannot even attest that one day we will know all the answers, so we certainly cannot be sure we will ever be able to inertly act with a perfect knowledge of them. As such, it might well be necessary to keep laws regarding murder as stringent as they are now, even if they negatively impact on the will of some to end their lives with assistance.[47] Similarly, without laws regarding equality and fairness (which, undoubtedly, society is still a long way from perfecting) we could lose track of what is rational altogether.

I will touch more upon the practical issues and subjects we should be considering most fervently later on. But it is important to consider morality as a form of science, remember. That means we need laws, communities of moral scientists with which to peer review theories and rational analysis to create solutions to complex problems. Science doesn't work on an act-by-act basis, and there is no reason to suppose that it would be better placed doing so.

---

[47] Please note that I am not saying the laws regarding murder are correct here, or that euthanasia should be made much easier. I am neither qualified nor practically informed enough to come down on either side. I raise this as a practical example, not as a personal opinion of what should happen in either case, and I apologise in advance if anyone views it as a shot against their knowledge, as that was not my intention.

What do rational moral facts look like?

Earlier on I was very critical of the idea of classical moral realism, and particularly the idea of independent moral facts which our moral intuitions are somehow uncovering. The whole thing reeks of fantasy in the same way as things like religious beliefs do, but moral facts may well exist in some way once we have created moral science.

Morality is a complex area of study, one where an interest in one moral principle can often lead to a conflict on a seemingly matching principle. So the best way to decipher how we can best create a rational and consistent theory of morality is to draw out exactly what the most basic, agreeable moral principles are that we want to take. How do we get these? Well, the easiest way is to think about exactly what the most basic values at stake in different political or moral preferences are. For instance, take the largely American belief in the right to gun ownership; many proponents would state this as a basic 'right', yet it is far from a basic moral principle. Underpinning it, instead, are the desires to be free/autonomous and the desire for protection. Were the person to not believe in either their own freedom, or else their own protection, it seems implausible that their belief in a right to gun ownership could be as strong.

There appear to be, at the very basic level, three values which all others seem to stem back to. It is our belief in these, for ourselves and our friends, which seem to drive all other moral concerns:

A desire to be free/have autonomy. This is about being able to make choices for oneself and one's immediate family/friends, without intervention or restriction.

A desire to have one's important interests protected. This is about being able to live without significant risk of being murdered or tortured.

A desire for fairness. This is to not be treated less well than, or receive less privileges than, others.

Arguably, there are two other strong basic principles, but these appear to stem from the first three. I note them here for clarity of them being important secondary principles:

A desire to be listened to. To not have one's values ignored in wider society. Arguably, this is a mixture of autonomy, protection and fairness concerns.

A desire to thrive. To be able to live life how one wishes to live life (pursue jobs, movement, entertainment, etc., as one wishes). Arguably this is also a mixture of the first three.

The adoption of these first three/five moral principles allows us to create and examine moral facts in the real world. If we want a rational policy on gun control, for example, we must weigh it in relation to the effect it has on these founding principles. Are our rules stamping on our personal autonomy? Are they endangering individual protection? Are they allowing people to be treated fairly, and to thrive? Moreover, do the minor interests of the many trample on the major interests of the few – and if so, how do we ensure democratic systems safeguard the major interest of the few?

Of course this doesn't make the decision suddenly easy: I chose gun control as it is one of the more complex decisions a society can make policies on. A decision to unfairly restrict it can leave many feeling completely without personal thriving, and in some circumstances leaving them feeling unprotected or controlled. Whilst a decision to allow guns to be sold too easily can do exactly the same; it can lead to high levels of gun crime, definite assaults on personal freedom and thriving, a feeling of fear in the population and an unfairness to those who can't afford the level of protection which everyone else is now walking around armed with.

However, adopting rational moral principles like these do have a distinct advantage: we no longer have to back our moral or political decisions with regards to old books or pieces of paper, or even to authority figures or tradition. Instead, we can debate and analyse, use statistics of gun deaths and facts about gun ownership, perhaps even examples of places where each have been tried, to rationally educate and make better decisions. And, what's more, whilst there will still be unhappy people at most decisions society makes, one at least has the transparency of showing how the decision is made based upon that person's own basic values. Those who are unhappy can offer debate and reason, rather than contributing blindly and wanting to force opinions so often.

The adoption of rational moral principles like these are not – like current societal laws – the gradual, unguided growth of laws over the ages. Neither are they – like philosophical theories – the adoption of moral laws which some set of philosophers deem 'best' due to their own moral whims and feelings. Instead, these moral principles are drawn from the principles that actual people have, from the political policies that we all actually support, and from the hopes and fears we each individually have. This, more than most, is a theory of morality for the people, and drawn from the people. Current mistakes in political or moral laws are often deemed as authoritarian or otherwise forced by those suffering from it, as they are simply passed down from a leader or party who wishes to install them on society. This is not the case with a theory which is drawing conclusions logically from people's own basic moral values.

Rational morality is about extending moral principles rationally, from an agreed and rational base, in the interests of the people who actually live in society.

Chapter 3: Defending a Rational Theory of Morality

In the following chapter I'll briefly discuss some potential criticisms of the theory which I developed in chapter 2, with the intention of testing its legitimacy.[48] I will state each in its most persuasive form, as I see it, and then discuss how it affects a rational theory of morality.

People are unmoved by rationality

There are many studies claiming to indicate that people are best moved by emotional wording or emotional accounts of immoral events than they are by hearing the rational reasons why such events are wrong. They claim to show that people are better moved by emotional ideas in general than rational ones.[49] Undoubtedly, many will state this shows a rational version of morality to be wrong.

---

[48] Some of the main criticisms were dealt with in the explanation of the theory in Chapter 2. For example, the problem of figuring why we ought to be rational in the first place, or why rationality means we should be moral at all. The criticisms I explain are further ideas which have been bought to my attention through discussion or contemplation on this issue.

[49] One of these was noted in the last chapter: Slovic, P. (2007). "If I look at the mass I will never act": Psychic numbing and genocide. Judgement and Decision Making, 2(2), 79-95. However, many studies claim to prove that either rationality isn't a good motivator, or even that rational people are less moral. Check here for some examples: http://www.hoover.org/publications/policy-review/article/6577.

This is not a good criticism of what I have written as it assumes that because rationality is the basis of morality then emotion is no longer important. This is not a necessary belief of rational morality. I have argued that traditional moral realism is wrong as it assumes the existence of independent moral facts, and that these don't exist. Thereby it is irrational to hold people to rules based around fantastical but ultimately flawed notions of morality, however well they motivate people.

Although being rational is certainly the key to uncovering the truth this doesn't mean that emotion can't be used to advocate different moral causes. I may even believe that everyone should be trained to think rationally, perhaps having advanced mathematical or formal logic education built into the curriculum of the schooling system, but this does not mean that advocating with the use of emotion before this happens is wrong. It also doesn't mean that emotion is somehow unimportant; emotion being an entirely rational, evolutionarily formed reaction. I would never argue that emotional reactions themselves are irrational, and I don't believe it could successfully be done.

What is wrong, however, is using emotion to bully people into irrational beliefs, or using it to decide what is the best course of events *against* an answer posed by rationality. For example, my theory would argue against a political party who were using emotional tactics to elicit reactions against an event or occurrence which was not immoral. This undoubtedly occurs often in countries where religion still holds a prime place in government, like in the USA, and can be demonstrated with reference to the commonplace, irrational arguments against gay marriage, amongst others. The fact that rationality doesn't motivate people currently is not a good criticism of my theory; indeed the probability that this theory may well turn out to be controversial would be down to the fact that rationality is currently devalued in society. The importance of the ideas that have compelled me to write about rational ethics implicitly note that rationality is not currently a good widespread motivator, and the reason that I am writing this is partly to support that it should become one ahead of religious and basic emotional appeal. The likes of republican positions against gay marriage are actually prime candidates for exemplifying this kind of problem: we are told that gay marriage 'devalues' traditional marriage, or that it is 'unnatural', or even worse that it is against 'God's will'. These are not good arguments, but the emotional pull of terms like 'natural' or 'God's will' and the threatening sentiment of gay marriage 'devaluing' one's own, are tailor-made to be threatening to US culture. They do not actually make a great deal of sense, but primarily consist of emotional puppetry.

We should look at how exactly we do use emotion in every area though, not just in politics. Well-known particle physicist Brian Cox is famed for believing that we need to open science to the masses: "If we can persuade enough people that science is as wonderful as it is useful, then we will be far better equipped as a civilization to face the great challenges of the 21st century."[50] Many would take his principle further, to mean that we need to use emotive language and relate science to people in the real world, outside of academia. This, too, is absolutely necessary. However, with an area like rational morality, this gets messy, as it allows people to bring in emotion rather than rationality. Again, like with the example of politics in the USA: you can have one political party arguing for gay marriage, one arguing against it, and all kinds of

---

[50] http://blogs.wsj.com/speakeasy/2012/02/20/why-quantum-theory-is-so-misunderstood/

emotional ploys on both sides with no reliance on facts. The development of morality as a science, and of a scientific community dedicated to developing facts and ideas related to morality, would be of great benefit to reducing this irrational way of ruling societies. Like how we should be turning to evidence when we discuss science, we should do the same with morality.

Emotion isn't necessarily a worry, though. We find it easy, for example, to differentiate between scientific fact and the emotive language we might use to describe scientific facts. For instance, stars don't really 'give birth' to things, and no one appears to be under the illusion that this means certain objects are children of the stars in any meaningful manner. No one is suing celestial objects for alimony. But with morality we are dealing with how we should act, not how things do act. As a result, we are bound to be faced by new problems, and one of these may well be the mixing of emotive, advocacy language and moral facts. This is an area to be mindful of. At current, we especially need to be wary that it's likely the language of morality and its inability to describe things rationally which puts people off moral ideas as an objective subject. People view emotion as personal and subjective (which it is) so if we speak in emotional terms about morality, it might have the immediate effect of garnering donations for certain causes, but it isn't likely to foster a long-term understanding of morality as being objective.

Valuing what is natural to us

Fantastical ideas like classic moral realism relate to people on some surface level, but they realistically distance people from morality by putting it out there as some unknowable source. As a result it has led to high levels of understanding morality as an entirely relativist concept;

actions of moral intent seem to have become more of an ambiguous, personal matter or else of forced legal/social obligation, than something of real, solidly understood value.

Take wildlife conservation, for example. The World Wildlife Fund (WWF) is one of the world's largest charities, yet it is difficult to see exactly how rational it is. It often aims to help endangered species, yet these species are becoming extinct in the modern world because, for whatever reason, they no longer have a place to thrive. The WWF is so successful at eliciting donations because it shows individual, magnificent looking animals in its adverts, and appeals both to our senses of awe and compassion, as well as to our sense of not wanting to lose things 'forever'. Such campaigns appeal to an uninformed sense of 'what if we need the panda at a later time?! It will be gone!'

Criticism of such charities is met by fierce complaints from patrons, who mount the criticism as coldly rational and uncompassionate. They are right, but only because compassion and warmth instead of rationality would be counter-productive in this instance. Their response, though, is the equivalent of children's charities defending our will to ignore the masses at the expense of the one child.[51] The WWF does not save pandas because it believes pandas are sentient and it cares for their well-being. It cares for pandas out of misplaced guilt that there is no longer a place for them in the world, or perhaps even out of misunderstanding the reason pandas can no longer exist naturally (because we have destroyed their habitats, not because we need to gather them into zoos, etc.) If the WWF were being rational, it would be every bit as concerned for pigs or cows who are sentient and die in their millions every day simply because we find frivolous, irrational reasons to

---

[51] Slovic, P. (2007).

disrespect their interests (mainly out of that same irrational 'survival of the fittest' belief that we are top of the food chain, and so have no reason to be anything but cold and calculated in the direction of other species – see chapter 6). Realistically, the WWF is not valuing the interests of sentient individuals – either in terms of saving individuals based on their sentience, or conserving the environment for these individuals to live in – but is valuing an abstract concept that has run away with its own success. The organisation has become so good at soliciting donations and functioning as a business that its economic interest in surviving as a company now outweighs its interests to look inward and realise it is largely doing little of moral value.

What the WWF (and its position in society as a respected charity) shows us is that even those moral causes we currently have in society are almost entirely borne out of ignorance, to the degree that we should question each and every one of them as to the point of their existence at all. If we are each respecting the interests of every other sentient individual in the first place, what is the point of most charity? And until we get to that stage, why shouldn't every charity be focused on simply creating a respect for sentience full stop, as a method to get there? The list of questions we need to ask is huge if we begin being rational about explicit moral movements like charities, and these are but two of them.

The idea of rational morality agrees with Harris in stating that morality is about the well-being of sentient individuals. And in doing so it not only has logic on its side, it also creates a morality of simplistic beauty with which we can reduce every one of these ambiguous causes into nothingness, and instead form an over-arching rational meaning, which actually gives purpose to moral causes rather than individual pressure groups. We may still need some charities, sure, but a charity to appease every person's moral guilt so they themselves don't have to recognise the most important ones (those that respect the starving or the homeless, or the billions of farm animals), in favour of their personal aesthetic taste in *liking* tigers? That's irrational and it simply must go; we're doing nothing but pummelling our rational abilities into a tiny box which we can hide away in order to follow our gut instincts. These are charities of a time when religious, personal spirituality ruled the earth, and many of them likely no longer have a place under their current guises.

Similarly, with simplicity comes motivation. It's no wonder people are not currently motivated to be moral. Merge the fact that so many ambiguous charities and moral causes exist (our wide-ranging charity scene reflects personal tastes, rather than the interests of the needy) with the fact that the current moral landscape is entirely inept at giving anyone a truthful reason to act morally in the first place, and we have an astoundingly hopeful reason to start throwing our support behind a rational form of morality. This theory will not just be relevant to those with strong moral intuitions, it will also be of relevance to those who want to live in and understand reality, and I've yet to see a compelling reason how anyone, anywhere falls outside of this group. Even religious and spiritualist individuals are so because they believe they have rational reason to be. This theory, despite being heavily critical of such belief systems, should provide an excellent challenge in asking why they need to hold these beliefs anymore, and further in challenging any 'experiential truths' which they think are currently relevant. People are spiritual because it is functional for them to be so. This theory takes most of that remaining functionality away and clears the path for rational thinking and collaborative morality to merge properly.

Rationality is a patriarchal concept

Postmodern subsets of feminism often argue against ideas like rationality, as it is said to be a concept of male importance, forced by patriarchal hands.[52] Despite the sexism of assuming that women are not as naturally rational as men (nothing could be further from the truth, as the capacity and tendency to be rational is equal in both sexes), it is that same paradoxical argument that was encountered earlier, the one that goes "Why assume rationality as a base value?", whilst systematically assuming rationality as its base value, and being unable to assume otherwise.

One can argue against a notion that says 'we ought to speak English' with an argument in English, because other equally valid languages exist, and more languages can even be formulated which hold the same level of meaning as English does. One cannot argue against the importance of rationality whilst using rationality, though, precisely because there is no other option of formulating an alternative for truth finding.[53] Rationality is so necessary that it doesn't even make sense to

---

[52] This is a general point of contention among this area of feminism in society. Individual feminists who argue similar points include: Lloyd, G, *The Man of Reason: "Male" and "Female" in Western Philosophy* (1984)

[53] Many times I have seen the solution of alternative forms of truth finding touted as being that of adding emotion into the process (for example Bryan Luke in 'Taming Ourselves or Going Feral? Toward a Nonpatriarchal Metaethic of Animal Liberation'). It's not clear how one could even create such a process which valued both rationality and emotion, without basically subjecting the rational system to all kinds of bias, yet this kind of postmodern argument doesn't seem overly concerned about its lack of rational consistency. In

assume it is not a base value. Not just in morality, but in everything. And a premise that purports we ought to be rational is assuming the very least that we must assume, and no more. Remember, stating we need rationality for truth finding is no different to stating that we need to find truth in order to be truth finding.

This postmodern criticism itself is one that misunderstands the rationale behind appropriating rationality a place of value. It is assumed that because a woman's classic role in society is one of emotional strength, it is therefore the opposite of rationality. This doesn't hold true with what we know about rationality now. Emotions are intensely rational reactions that occur in relation to events in the real world. Responding with disgust to something you find disgusting is no less rational than responding with no specific reaction to something you have no conscious interest in. This criticism is based on prejudices from a bygone era – that men are rational and women emotional. A baseless claim that cannot be taken seriously.

There is undoubtedly truth to the claim that sexism is a problem in society, and it's through this that we see where the postmodern feminist criticism has taken a wrong turn. Society still seems to deem women as less important than men, studies still find women to make less money than men for performing the same roles, and women are primarily portrayed as sexual or domestic objects in advertisements

---

a bygone era, ideas which used rationality to criticise rationality might fall down as soon as analysis shows it to be irrational, yet postmodern studies seem to thrive simply by denouncing rationality as somehow prejudice (more claims which are questionable and currently evidence-less). Unsurprisingly, scientists have begun to speak up against this kind of non-sensical postmodernism, the first I was aware of being Paul Gross and Norman Levitt's wonderful but now dated 'Higher Superstition: The Academic Left and it's Quarrels With Science' in 1994/98.

while men are reduced to nowhere near the same level of objectification.

There is also little doubt that this social problem of sexism causes an issue for a good many areas of science, as scientific institutions are still open to indulging sexism given that they are run by people who live in what still appears to be a sexist society. But this kind of analysis, which agrees with feminist theory on the level of social prejudice, does not amount to a criticism of rationality or scientific method. Indeed, if we subject morality to the same rigours of reason as other forms of science, like I have argued that we should, then sexism is impossible to justify due to it being a prejudice as blatantly immoral as racism. Allowing this permission for rationality to penetrate morality would fight that very same patriarchal-led sexism that feminists abhor. Far from being patriarchal, a fair analysis shows rationality to oppose prejudice, and formulates the very argument that feminists use in order to grab progress. Opposing rationality in morality is paradoxical and incredibly self-defeating for feminism.

It is rational to be selfish, not moral?

I have already briefly argued against this idea in the previous chapter, but it is of significance here for several reasons. The first point to note is that altruism is also rational. 'Survival of the fittest' in the 'most selfish wins' type was understood, for a long time, to be the rational view of how things are, and this outdated concept very much informs this exact criticism. However, with what we now know about evolution, and about the nature of society, it is simply untrue to say that pure selfishness is an intelligent phenomenon; we know that it isn't, at least among humans. There may be incidences in which one is forced to practice self-defence, for example, and thus be 'selfish' in order to protect oneself. But this is not a general rule about society, and indeed it doesn't make sense to say that selfishness is the ideal rational state when working in mutually fulfilling collectives, such as societies. To posit this is to misunderstand rationality past a shallow level. If we are to accept morality as useful and truth based, like a science, we must make it rational. That's a simple claim which, as previously discussed, is well supported by the evidence.

Spiritual roots

In my time as an advocate in animal ethics, I came across many spiritually minded moral advocates with whom I've discussed rationalism and ethics. All seem to see rationality as somehow separate from ideas like kindness and compassion, as if they are simply not compatible. I have so far attempted to show that this is not the case (kindness and compassion spring from rational thinking; they are far from segregated), but this occurrence shows us a great deal about the roots of spiritual ideas.

Undoubtedly, many people, if not all, are instilled with moral intuitions. As we have seen, we are products of a rich evolutionary history, and tools like altruism have caused these intuitions because they are of great survival value. We intuitively needed to act morally in the past in order to survive in society. It is the media portrayal of the rational as somehow 'cold' or 'calculating' that is likely a big factor behind people's dismissal of rationality from being of moral use. The idea that rationality doesn't respect personal intuitions, and so is immoral, has in turn caused this. Rationality is seen to be critical of religion and personal spiritual beliefs, so given the implication up to now that these

70

things are markers of moral concepts like well-being, kindness and compassion, whilst rationality is seen to be a marker of cold calculation, it goes hand in hand that a desire to be moral and do what's right is tied up in inclinations for the spiritual and the religious rather than the rational.

We need look no further than the media for examples of the problem. Pushing the norms of society, the media posits characters like Dr. House from the hugely successful TV serial *House M.D*, or Counter Terrorist Agent Jack Bauer from the equally well-known *24*, in order to tell us what rational people are like. These characters famously tend away from close relationships, make cutthroat decisions and go off the rails in their often bizarre personal lives. A fair assessment would note that House and Bauer are rationally minded when it comes to their jobs, or gaining results in single-minded missions, but fairly irrational and incompetent with the way they treat other people, or with situations which are more complex than to involve immediate results. It makes for excellent TV, undoubtedly, but not such a great advert for rationality. These are society's rational role models, and no one would want to champion rationality based on their often disastrous lives and relationships.

This leads to some interesting conclusions, though. Spiritual beliefs may be delusions, but they exist because of (not in spite of) the desire to be rational. There is an evolutionary and culturally inbuilt sense that morality is important, and the desire to be spiritual comes from the desire to recognise this as well as scientific rationality (which we are also inbuilt to respect). These two things thus seem very separate until it is pointed out in clear, certain terms that morality *is* rational. Once we do this we can see spirituality in a fresh new light; not as some form of random irrational tendency, but rather as desperation to understand the world, and a desire not to be pigeonholed by a scientific method of looking at the world which is marketed as being cold and neutral on the subject of morality. Morality, which on a very basic level appears to be incompatible with our rational inclinations, is hardwired into us because it is so rationally useful. We thus strive to reject rationality as a moral cause because the evidence we think we are aware of (primarily evidence in the media, or else in philosophy books) shows us that rationality is incompetent at judging morality.

Not only does this help to explain spirituality as a rational matter, it also provides an easy way for people with spiritual beliefs to see past them. Spirituality is not necessary, and need not be invented or promoted in order to have morality. We settle for spirituality because of our natural desire to be both rational and altruistic, the latter being a form of rationality which we are told isn't rational, and so we invent spiritual ideas to, in a sense, oppose rationality. But we no longer need spiritual 'experiential truth' in order to make morality valuable. Once we can show morality to be an important scientific discipline, the need for spiritual explanations, like the need for religion, can gradually fade away. The ability to see these spiritual experiences and morality both as rationally caused traits makes them no less wonderful to behold. We can experience the complexity of our rational abilities, and even those of vampire bats or other animals, whilst wondering at how an amazingly adept process such as evolution could have instilled them within us. Every part of this is inspiring. In fact, wondering at the complexity of reality in this way seems much more satisfying than wondering at the perceived randomness/arbitrary unknowability that spiritual explanations offer.

This leads us on to one of the great uses of rational morality. In clearing the need for spirituality we can outwardly remove it as a necessity of any kind, and thus show up the problems with it: the main one being that spirituality is born out of faith, which in turn is another word for prejudice.

This is not a description of any person of faith, but rather it is a definition of the concept of faith, and a plea for people who currently hold belief and value in faith to see the moral problems with it. I'm not referring only to those who believe in a formally recognised faith (like that of organised religion), but also those who claim to have personal experience of a 'god' or an 'energy' that simply cannot be proved. Human beings are not rational machines, and we find it easy to trick ourselves into comforting beliefs. In fact, we can explain our tendency to do this back to our evolutionary history.[54]

The reason to forgo faith, and its corresponding religious and spiritual beliefs, is thus not just a result of direct rationality but also a matter of moral motivation. A society that values faith implicitly values beliefs that are formed with no evidence, and ergo promotes the idea that this is a positive or acceptable way to form moral values. Anyone who disagrees with prejudice like racism, sexism or homophobia, must understand the structural problem with prejudice straight away, as it is formed in exactly the same way as a faith, and values a method of forming beliefs that doesn't require rationality or proof. Faith works in *exactly* the same way as prejudice, and whilst faith isn't always going to (and might not often, even) result in prejudice, a society which values,

---

[54] See: *Why We Believe in God(s). A Concise Guide to the Science of Faith.* J. Anderson Thomson Jr, MD, with Clare Aukofer.

defends and promotes faith-based thinking is implicitly going to do the same to prejudice. Both are formed without need for evidence or rationality and, as a result, both will flourish in a society in which either is rampant. If we consider religion to be a sunflower growing in the organic compost of faith, then we had better be ready for the weeds of prejudice as well.

One can partly disagree with this (i.e. show religious people often value forms of anti-prejudice, or show other causes of discrimination that don't breed faith), but as a structural matter the two are inseparable, and so we can assert that as a general matter both will flourish in the same conditions. There is no better example than my favourite one of American politics (sorry to any Americans reading this: I am not purposefully discriminating, yours is simply a well-known situation). Only a country which values religion can have arguments in which one side believes the marriages of other people (homosexuals) will destroy their own (religious republicans), and further, believe that regardless of having no evidence to back it up. There is absolutely no logic to this, and it's a classic form of people believing anything you tell them because you both want the same thing. In this case the tradition of marriage to be purely between straight people. The onus is on us to begin making the connection between faith and prejudice as a practical matter. We've no need to value faith as a way to be moral anymore, so there's no need to take the risk. Most problems of prejudice in society will appear completely unrelated to religion or spirituality, and as a direct causation they certainly are. Yet they both breed from a valuing of faith, and it's difficult to argue against this given that we know exactly similar events will almost certainly occur in exactly similar circumstances.

Scientists are rational, but they are often not moral

So, it is claimed, if science is about being rational, and scientists are not particularly moral, why should we believe morality is rational? In many ways one assumes this criticism comes from the exact understanding people see on TV: again, Dr. House is a marvellous scientific mind on medicine, but is far from exemplary in his social life and to his colleagues. Thus, rational people are known to be cold and immoral, and the circle completes as people who study science feel compelled to be cold and neutral about morality (as it is the way their role models behave), whereas people who study morality become suspicious of science. Before we even begin, we must note this: it is the case that currently many scientists do not submit to any good moral theory. Many, if not most, scientists still believe that science is mute on the subject of morality and, as a result, it's commonplace to see incidences of scientists also being religious or spiritual. Similarly, we see other scientists being neutral and relativist about it. This is to be expected and is by no means a criticism of a rational form of morality, which would disagree with both of these positions, instead favouring a third, more rational way for scientists to look at morality. We can't expect scientists (who are members of society) to act rationally on the subject of morality when we keep teaching the whole of society (including the scientists) that morality is an intensely non-rational or irrational occurrence.

Rationality doesn't 'make' scientists act rationally

This slightly different criticism is certainly compelling to some: that rationality doesn't even make scientists act rationally, so how compelling can it be? Yet, first of all, we can question whether all current science is even rational in the first place. The ideal of science certainly is

75

rationality, but much investigation that falls under the label of science at current might not even pass any tests of rationality. Science is primarily about testing hypotheses (informed beliefs that are held). And it might also be the case that some areas of science are more rooted in tradition than scientific reasoning. There might be a lot of 'Bad Science', so to speak, and indeed authors like Ben Goldacre[55] have made a career out of trying to dig these unscientific ideas out from under the umbrella of science.

But also, just because one's job is labelled as "a scientist", does not mean that one is necessarily rational in any other area of his/her life. Just as we know that many priests are not necessarily men of faith,[56] many scientists are not necessarily men of reason. Indeed, there is less call for scientists to be completely rational than there is for priests to be completely religious, given that priesthood is a lifestyle choice on top of a job, whereas science is mostly seen only as a job. So we'd expect the relationship to be more biased in terms of scientists deviating from their supposed roles. And, as I've stated, there is currently no recognised scientific form of morality to speak of; we are taught that morality is either spiritual in some way, or is relativist. The entire point of this theory is to make this case and encourage us all (including scientists) to acknowledge morality as a science.

Anyhow, scientific engagement can certainly be a result of a society that is solely valuing rationality, but it is also a result of any society that wants progress in any area of industry or medicine, for example.

[55] http://www.badscience.net/about-dr-ben-goldacre/
[56] As Daniel Dennet explained in his Christmas Essay for the New Statesman magazine 2011 entitled "The Social Cell" p 50-53. (19 Dec 11 – 1 January 12 edition)

So it doesn't make sense to judge the actions of scientists as the actions of the rational, as this would be the morality of current science and not the science of morality (the former being something that is entirely dependent on the society in which scientific investigation is taking place, and not necessarily a sign of what is rational). We cannot judge the ability of rationality to create consistent morality until we have a society, and scientific community, which values only rationality and is educated to accept that morality is an area of science like I am arguing in this theory. Until then, the scientists we see will be a reflection of the 'contain rationality to our jobs' types that society creates.

Many will refuse to be rational

Essentially this moral theory suffers the same problem as any moral theory. Many people simply don't care, and so will not begin valuing morality rationally. This doesn't mean the theory is wrong, it simply means that what needs to be done to advance it has to be creative and intelligent in its approach. Even evolution went through a stage of huge ridicule. However, I believe this theory stands a better chance than most, as a practical matter. It is less likely, in my mind, that people in increasingly secular societies will reject this theory than a fantastically created morality like religion or classical moral realism.

Chapter 4: A Science of Morality isn't About Numbers

Inherent, it seems, in all secular work on morality is the belief that it is about numbers, to some degree. It's the idea that if morality is to be considered rational in some way then we will eventually be able to create formulae for deciding what is best to do in any given situation.

Yet, as touched upon in the previous chapters, human beings are not good judges of morality as a rational matter. We have evolved through a rich history, but by no means have we become perfect. It does seem initially intuitive to think that as we progress – as we become more educated about the reality we inhabit – we will be much better placed to make these sorts of decisions. In the same way as we are all much better placed on thinking about the best ways to keep our family warm with our better, modern understanding of the laws of insulation, perhaps one day we will all be better placed to make ethical decisions in our everyday life with a better understanding of morality. After all, none of us could recite laws of insulation, but we all grasp the ideas such that we know that a blanket will help to keep us warmer than not having a blanket, and a functioning central heating system is better still.

So that may be, but to think of morality as a formulaic numbers game is to miss the point. It is not sensible to assume that we will ever be educated enough to make decisions like formulaic machines. A simple example should show why that is.

The 'medical emergency' similarity

Consider medical emergencies. Over the centuries our understanding of how the body works has increased dramatically. Even in as short a time period as two hundred years, we might look back in shock at the things doctors did in the name of improving our health or solving our medical problems. Disease was commonplace, and not just down to bad safety rules (like those which are mistakenly blamed for causing the spread of MRSA in modern hospitals[57]), but due to the lack of understanding we had regarding how diseases were spread, or how the human body works.[58]

As ever expanding as our knowledge of medicine is, most of us now have a better grasp. This stretches far beyond the hospital, and many of us (while not medical experts) would be able to provide basic first aid assistance. Similarly, we are much better able to avoid certain illnesses by knowing rules about health and safety, and about the basics of how disease spreads. But still, most of us would be ill-placed to perform heart surgery or a trachea bypass like surgeons or paramedics, respectively, could. Despite our growing societal understanding of internal medicine, this much has not changed and is not likely to.

---

[57] The science journalist Ben Goldacre, referenced so often in this book, writes an excellent piece on this subject in *Bad Science*, where he uncovers the fact that no MRSA has ever been found living on dirty mops or in dusty corners of hospitals – it is a myth that MRSA comes from dirty hospitals, and an unfortunate myth that the media completely promotes.

[58] Famously, for a long time we considered smell to be the thing that carried disease. Whilst this was scientifically understood at the time (as bad smells often do naturally alert us to dangerous things to avoid) we progressed to a better understanding of germs and bacteria, and as a result we can avoid diseases better with our knowledge that it isn't the smell itself that is problematic.

Indeed, it seems irrational to predict a time when all of us are educated to the degree in which we might be able to perform heart surgery. Furthermore, we don't consider this a problem, as we train people to fulfil that role in society. We should view morality in partly the same way, but with one notable exception – laws and rules should replace doctors and paramedics as the guides.

I think this is a fair analogy. With our growing understanding of medicine, each of us has become more informed, and our perspectives of potential danger have changed from, say, trying to stay away from smells (which were once thought to carry disease) to trying to neutralise harmful germs (which are the true carriers of disease). The same should be true of morality, and as we come to know more about how morality works (in its rational role) so we should all be able to live our lives making more informed decisions. But as this improves, we should be comfortable knowing that we need moral rules, like we need heart surgeons. We are not all ever going to be well placed to calculate formulas in real time as to the best moral decisions to make, in the same way as we are not all ever going to be educated to clear an artery. The complexities of modern life and the complexities of medical emergencies are similar, in this respect.

Failing to plan is planning to fail

I didn't think a saying of an old business studies teacher (which was shouted at me, through lesson after lesson, to explain the importance of business plans), would be cropping up in anything I'd write on the subject of morality, but here we are. It demonstrates the point perfectly: if we fail to plan for the kinds of individuals we are, then the kinds of individuals we are will ruin the best intentions we have. Or more succinctly, failing to plan is planning to fail.

I use the example of euthanasia often to illustrate a point where it might be a lesser of two evils to outlaw someone's ability to help another person to die. And yet I understand, perfectly well, that if one person wants to die there should be no reason – whatsoever – why the state should be morally allowed to intervene and stop a friend, family member or even a perfect stranger from helping them to do it. Indeed, it seems highly symptomatic of a society in the twilight of the grasp of religious tradition that groups might oppose suicide as a personal choice at all.

However, if it can be shown that allowing a rule to disregard murder on the grounds of euthanasia would allow for the murder of the elderly, or other dependant individuals – or in fact any individuals – against their will, then we need to strongly consider whether it is right to allow euthanasia.

I am not an expert on the 'ins and outs' of this case, and my personal opinion is that allowing for euthanasia under certain circumstances would not be problematic. However, I use this example to show a point – moral rules and their subsequent legal jurisdiction are required because human beings are not perfect rational agents. Murder happens, personal greed can overcome the rational decision-making process, etc., and facts like these have to be taken into account. Failing to plan for the imperfection of humans is, quite simply, planning to fail. It's nothing more than living in a fantasy world, casting away practical concerns in favour of holding onto theoretical ideas.

Shallow pragmatism

The atheist ethicist and author Peter Singer takes a position of utilitarianism, believing that suffering and pleasure are what matters, and that due to this we must make our decisions based on what will maximise pleasure and minimise suffering.[59] I have a lot of respect for Singer – he and I share some opinions in the subject of animal ethics, and also share much more on the subject of the need for secular ethics. I, however, do not agree with his position as a utilitarian.

The flaws in utilitarianism are many and well known. For instance, where do you draw the line when something like gang rape seemingly proves a moral act by maximising pleasure among many and causing only one person to suffer? Among many utilitarians suffering is therefore regarded as a graver thing to avoid than pleasure is to be caused, which makes utilitarianism an essential grasping on one fact rather than two – that suffering is meaningful and must be alleviated. Among other problems, this brings us back to the initial issue of moral realism, as it simply states there is a moral fact with little or no relevance to reality other than to our intuitions, or our behaviour.

In this respect, whether choosing Singer's utilitarianism, or any form of deontological (rule or rights based) moral realism instead, we are simply doing the moral equivalent of choosing between Christianity and Islam. There's no evidence on either side, just a will to believe in one rather than the other – a decidedly irrational choice in the first place, held up only by posturing from all sides upon which is the right answer.[60] This is a conflict which has been commonplace in religion

---

[59] *Practical Ethics*, Singer, P. 2nd Edition, 1993.
[60] *Animal Rights and Human Obligations*. Singer, P. and Regan, T. 1976.

for many years, and it should worry us as rationalists, since people debating made-up ideas which are supported only by 'intuitions' or 'ought-is deductions', are unlikely to bear truth.

Similarly, utilitarianism falls foul of exactly the problem which I discussed above – failing to plan. To assert utilitarianism successfully, despite all of its problems, one still has to assert certain moral rules (like making murder illegal), so in essence why bother with utilitarianism at all? It speaks to those parts of us which like to formulate and judge issues, sure, but aren't there better theories that do this? The theory of rational morality which I am arguing for certainly speaks to our rational intuitions, as well as to our will to formulate ideas. It suffers none of the problems of utilitarianism, as it doesn't make any unjustified or meta-physical claims about morality.

A reformed version of utilitarianism might accept that suffering is the thing we should be worried about, rather than putting so much value on pleasure. It might also agree with the idea of rights and of laws against indecent immoral acts. However, it is always going to miss the point – it subscribes to what I would call 'shallow pragmatism'.

What a rational morality asks us to do is think logically. We do not have evidence for deities setting rules, so let's ignore the idea of God-formed moral facts. We do not have evidence for independent moral facts at all, so let's ignore the idea of moral realism. We do, however, have evidence that morality is in some way rational, that we all seem to value morality, and therefore that we ought to be rational about it (in the most meaningful way in which we can speak of 'ought'), so let's discover what moral facts there are by using consistency and rationality, and by drawing decisions back to those three (or five) basic, shared ethical principles we summarised in chapter 2.

But utilitarianism, at its worst, asks us to think in a shallow pragmatic way whereby we must judge each act on each act's merits, or worse, judge morality by suffering, alone. This is failing to plan and is symbolic of a theory which misunderstands our human nature of not being perfect, rational machines. Furthermore, it asserts a 'fact' that suffering is the marker of morality. Of course, suffering is an important aspect of well-being, but boiling morality down to just this one principle makes no rational sense. We are back with the classic problems of moral realism when we hear such assumptions.

Earlier, I also considered the criticism: 'scientists aren't rational', which in a more fulfilling way might translate as 'people cannot be perfectly rational'. Whilst this isn't a problem for rational morality, it is a problem for act utilitarianism. Rule utilitarianism (which involves following the best rules in order for society to bring about the most good/least suffering) is slightly better than act utilitarianism (following the best decision to bring about the most good/least suffering in any single circumstance), in that it takes on board the nature of human beings as animals, rather than rational machines, yet it is still problematic. It holds at its centre the idea that when faced with a decision we must choose the best course of action based on the general rule that will create the most happiness. And yet, it still misses the point in a significant way: happiness doesn't sum up all that is to be considered about morality. There's no evidence that happiness could define morality better than well-being, and even if there were, we'd still be better placed deriving that evidence via rational morality – and by reference to the basic moral beliefs everyone holds – rather than via a blatant assumption.

Again, reformed versions of this theory take on board suffering *and* happiness. But that's all it ever is. Life is boiled down to two extremes, avoiding suffering and provoking happiness – two moral facts that do not exist independently, and for which there is no reason to believe they do. The idea I have put forth is, essentially, that we all agree on a definition of morality and then extend it logically – this is always going to be a better bet.

It might be argued that once one accepts rational morality, and the non-existence of independent moral facts, then rule utilitarianism (as explained) is fair game. But why? Why on earth do we need to think about life in this manner? Why do we need to make this about suffering and happiness, as two polar opposites – why not stick with the original definition of morality and make our rules based on the practical application of the well-being of sentient individuals in any given circumstance, weighing against three basic principles? We can still use ideas like minimising suffering and maximising pleasure, for instance, without reducing our entire theory and moral code to it (even if it turns out 99% of our moral code is to do with suffering and pleasure). A rational morality doesn't need to ever reduce to utilitarianism, unless in individual situations – in which case it isn't utilitarianism, it is a single equation or summing up based on similar factors to those which utilitarianism evokes wholesale.

It seems, certainly it has always seemed to me, that utilitarianism is fairly popular among ethicists because it plays to our intuitions about wanting to judge and formulate. It comes out best in exceptional thought experiments where we are posed the question that shows we would always do that which caused the least suffering or that which caused the most happiness. Yet it misses the point that the only moral concern should be well-being, and that suffering and happiness are aspects of this rather than the other way around. We live in a world where the well-being of sentient individuals (both humans and other animals) is routinely ignored, and where people seem to be happiest when choosing what the value of their own lives should be (without being told, from some meagre assessment, that it is 'suffering' to be avoided and 'pleasure' to be caused – and indeed without being forced to live by rules that establish this order). In fact, the two emotions (suffering and pleasure) interact on such a spectrum that they can often form in situations in which one directly causes the other.[61] Formulae that aim to be so precise in setting rules do not make sense given what we know about the mental states which it is aiming to either reduce or provoke, and only appear to make sense if we are to go back to the fantastical notion of 'independent moral facts' that state 'suffering should be avoided' – facts which can be shown not to exist.

Well-being, albeit a difficult to define concept itself is, as Harris states, no different to valuing 'health', which is a similarly hard to define concept. We don't need to reduce health to being about pain and pleasure, so there's no need to do so with ethics – not when well-being already does the job quite nicely. We can in fact amend what well-being involves if required, as science investigates further.

As a result, it makes sense to call the corresponding theory which looks at more than two precise mental states, and more than individual

---

[61] This is very much a philosophical point, but one which is built into our understanding of emotion. Imagine being given an ice cream right now. Taste good? Now imagine being starved, and kept from water for 3 days, then being given an ice cream. Taste even better? Of course it does. We are evolutionarily wired to get more pleasure from something we desperately need, than something we just want. Whilst it is ethically questionable to frustrate needs in order to cause greater pleasure, this kind of example does demonstrate that the two extremes of suffering and pleasure are not as unconnected as people think. They likely do not exist as two separate emotions, like we imagine, but rather as mental states which have an effect on one another.

decisions in individual circumstances, one of 'thorough pragmatism' –
a form of pragmatism which is based on rationality and so provable at
its very beginnings, without having to become shallow in its application
of valuing unknowable consequences. It is perhaps no surprise that a
solid form of 'thorough pragmatism' appears to be one and the same as
a scientific rational morality.

The rationalist's distraction – non-human animals

Although heavily referenced in the work of Singer and an increasing
number of secularist thinkers, rationalists appear to be heavily distracted from talking about non-human animals. In the rare instances
where they are discussed, prejudice and faith-based thinking call the
shots. Perhaps this comes from the long traditions which the western
world has had in believing animals do not have souls, or it could be
because of the rich, deontological tradition which has seen animals
denigrated to the status of unable participants in a contractual agreement to respect each other's rights. Who knows? The fact is that such
views of morality are no longer relevant, and animals are now on the
moral agenda.

The better angels of our nature

Steven Pinker's recent analysis of the historical decrease in violence,[62]
leading to our being able to confidently state that we now live in a more
peaceful world than ever before, is one of the 21st century's great
achievements of literature so far. It is wonderful in showing something
this book is indebted to: the idea that as we tend toward and become

---

[62] *The Better Angels of Our Nature.* Pinker, S. 2011.

more rational (or as Pinker puts it, as we 'extend reason'), we also become more peaceful and civilised. I believe Pinker is mistaken in one respect, in that he believes one of the major causes is how empathy has been rationally extended, whereas I believe empathy itself is a symptom of rationality. We've no need to attribute the cause of a more peaceful world to empathy, so much as to increasing rationality (of which empathy is a natural part), but this isn't a philosophical book review of Pinker's otherwise excellent analysis, and so I will leave that discussion for another time.

Pinker's analysis of violence focuses less on animals than humans, though, despite the history of humanity imparting more violence on other animals (which still sits at an astounding 1 trillion animals a year – including aquatic animals – as a conservative estimate[63]) than other humans. In just a single year one could be confident in the claim that we commit more violence against other animals than we *ever have* against human beings. The numbers are huge. The focus on humans shows something important – we like to add animals into moral equations as a rational matter, praising ourselves for our ability to remove our religious forefathers' irrational ideas, but we don't like to treat them to the levels of equality which, rationally speaking, their traits deserve. Perhaps a problem of our own 'shallow pragmatic' making.

Indeed, despite the issues in Peter Singer's work, it might be claimed that he is the only well-known rationalist to academically

---

[63]   http://fishcount.org.uk/fish-welfare-in-commercial-fishing/estimate-of-fish-numbers. The number of aquatic animals killed alone is said to be in the trillions, however this figure is truly unknowable as these animals are measured in tons rather than individual lives. Around 60 billion land animals are said to be killed each year but, again, this figure moves around and is truly unknowable. What we do know for sure is that these figures are unimaginably high.

admit the equality of other animals in issues like suffering, stating as he does that, "All the arguments to prove man's superiority cannot shatter this hard fact: in suffering the animals are our equals."[64]

Pinker's mistake in this (which is forgivable as an academic matter, given the focus on human history in education, though perhaps not forgivable as an ethical matter) may not disprove his theory, as it might still turn out that despite our horrendous, continuing exploitation of other animals, it is no worse than it used to be. So when adding to this calculation the 'better' state of inter-human violence, then we may well have definitely been in progress towards peace. However, it shows that we are wholly distracted when it comes to other animals – the one big, hidden prejudice of our time is most definitely 'speciesism'. And given our human penchant for the irrational (do you know anyone who doesn't indulge religion, spirituality or moral realism in some form?), it is ironic that we largely excuse our exploitation of sentient individuals in other species with the excuse that *they* aren't rational.

The utilitarian mistake – welfarism as a marker of 'betterness'

Pinker's comments on animals are backed up by beliefs in 'welfarism'. This constitutes our concern for the welfare of other animals which has resulted in laws that have cropped up in modern society, as well as facts like how we no longer burn cats or regularly exploit animals in frivolous forms of entertainment. So he believes that, all other things being equal, this kind of analysis constitutes an improvement for non-humans. But, this belief is a common mistake. Evidence shows Pinker

---

[64] *Animal Liberation.* Singer, P. 1975.

and Singer to be incorrect in their assumptions about welfare reform, from which Singer has made a career by championing, and which Pinker uses to erroneously back up his theory that things are now better for animals.

Legal scholar and animal rights theorist Gary L. Francione has been making the case against welfare reform, on moral and practical grounds, since the early 90s. We can reject his theory of 'animal rights' itself on the basis of its insistence, like most others, on using classical moral realism. Francione has made it clear in various places that he doesn't agree rationality is any sort of guarantor of morality, and believes science has nothing to say about morality. Similarly, it must be noted that his insistence on animals having just the one right, not to be used as property, is based on the idea that it is simply an independent moral fact that we must not exploit other animals (or sometimes he quotes the moral fact of non-violence). I reject this on the grounds that it is classical moral realism, much like Singer's.

However, Francione's work on the practical side of welfare reform is of immense importance. In *Animals, Property and The Law*,[65] Francione makes several breakthroughs in his legal examination of welfare reform. He notes, firstly, that animals are legally seen as property, and any attempt to improve the welfare of property has to be done by summing up the effect on current persons – i.e. human beings. Attempts to improve animal welfare (take PETA gaining partial success in getting chain restaurants to slaughter chickens in more humane ways[66]) have to be done by making it seem more economically efficient. As a

---

[65] *Animals, Property and the Law*. Francione, G. L. 1995.
[66]http://www.peta.org/features/the-case-for-controlled-atmosphere-kill-ing.aspx

result, not only do the animal groups, like PETA who are pushing for the changes, have to find success through earmarking economic improvements for companies in producing the animal products, they also can only be successful in getting improvements which do not cost more than the improvement is economically bringing in. As a result, though theoretically possible to improve animal welfare this way, welfarism as an idea is incredibly limited in affording protection to animals. The real way to improve their conditions is to grant them a legal status akin to persons, rather than property, and we simply can't do this while we societally see them as products to be utilised for our consumption.

I will further discuss the practical limits of welfarism later in the book, however, this idea is almost entirely missed in Singer's, and in Pinker's, work. There is an assumption that these welfare regulations are 'better' for animals, but the truth is that there is little evidence for this. Indeed, from Francione's work we *know* that the individual welfare regulation that groups like PETA pick isn't due to its ability to significantly improve the lives of animals, but more down to the case PETA can make for industry taking the change on board – the regulation is picked solely because of its economic efficiency and thus potential for success (sometimes referred to as 'picking the low hanging fruit'). Yet as far as PETA are concerned, with their policy of 'animals are not ours to use', improving a company's ability to use animals efficiently is neither a smart move nor a rational one.

Add to this the fact that all of these large, successful animal groups are essentially businesses, in which their survival to 'fight for the animals' depends on their ability to create success by picking economically efficient welfare regulations, thus garnering donations for continued activity through such public success, and it soon becomes apparent that welfare regulation is not as 'for the animals' as it seems. Individuals creating the campaigns are employed by the groups for their ability to create successes, and successes themselves are manufactured through economically efficient arguments. It becomes difficult to see at what point the regulation campaigns are being judged by their ability to improve things for animals at all, as the volunteers (who do pretty much what the business executives say) are the only ones appearing to value the animals' interests, and they are not the ones who create the policies. There appears to be an unbreakable, ineffective circle in progress.

Furthermore, all welfarism rests on the philosophical assumption that animals simply *are* helped by welfare regulation, on a conceptual scale of betterness which no one seems able to create. Given Francione's mountain of legal examination, the lack of holding animal groups to such a real scale is worrying, especially when we know animal charities are erring into irrationality (as earlier discussed regarding the WWF). So, more work obviously needs to be done in the area if Pinker's claim is to hold any water.

But let's also think about non-human animal interests a little. It's a subject I have some experience of, having grown up on an egg farm. We had one big shed with around three quarters 'free range-hens' and one quarter 'barn hens'. The difference between the two labels in terms of consumer confidence is huge, and indeed advocates like Singer see legislation regarding free-range eggs as some of the most significant improvements for animals, ever.[67] Yet, as a young teenager growing up on a hen farm with both free-range and non-free-range, I hope I can

---

[67] A point Francione references and takes Singer to task on here. Singer's ideas appear philosophically sound, but it is the legal detail and practical theory that brings him crashing down to Earth. http://www.abolitionistapproach.com/replacing-one-cage-with-another/

be forgiven for stating that for non-human animals the differences are miniscule at best. 'One big cage' is really the only way to look at free-range, as opposed to a smaller one or lots of little ones for non-free-range. The 'betterness' is very definitely in the heads of humans and marketing executives, and also unexplainably in the work of some rationalist ethicists.

The reason for this difference between industrial reality and consumer perception is that welfarism, as well as relying on rationally unsound utilitarianism (PETA's 'animal rights philosophy' is actually the 'animal welfare' philosophy championed by Singer, if you examine it), rests on very human concepts. One will often hear an advocate for free-range or 'humane' alternatives to regular animal products saying things like 'If I was a farmed chicken, I'd be grateful for the extra room'. But a chicken can't have these thoughts, not in any way similar to that which is being expressed. A chicken, to our knowledge, does not form mental coping mechanisms based on the assumption that 'it could be worse'. Indeed, don't we think this is a uniquely human characteristic, based on some fairly advanced forms of rational thinking – or at least shouldn't we, until proven otherwise? So why are we making the argument as if a chicken would think in this way? Welfarism, despite its speciesist results, is built on decidedly anthropomorphic and unscientific assumptions. On the one hand, champions of welfarism criticise more 'extreme' forms of 'animal rights' (like veganism) for anthropomorphism, and yet they use the same reasoning in justifying their own beliefs.

What should be obvious about any mammals, and even certain groups of mentally impaired humans, is that they do not necessarily form coping mechanisms. They may get used to suffering, but this doesn't mean they will suffer any less as time goes on. Even if they do form coping mechanisms, as far as we know they do not have the conceptual ability to theorise in a way such as 'Well, it's bad in here but at least I'm not in this exact spot, but in a smaller cage, or closer to the other hens in this already small shed'. So why do we assume that by removing the cage, but replacing it with a bigger cage (shed) just crammed with lots more birds (maybe increasing the space allowed the chicken by an inch, or even ten inches) it would be better? One thing animals share with humans is a rich variety of interests, and slightly increasing one of them in this way will likely have no psychological benefits for a rationally less capable individual like a chicken. It screams to our human will to formulate and adjudge 'betterness', as does utilitarianism as a whole, but it appears to do little if anything for the non-human animal. Theoretical kings with no practical substance.

We must also take on board the stark fact – which we are also indebted to Francione for – that the animals currently in sheds will never experience the higher welfare regulation themselves. Animals on farms live from maybe a few months to 5 years,[68] whereas welfare regulation takes many more years than this to come into force (due to the earlier mentioned legal and economic problems – governments must give businesses time to implement changes as animals are not persons, they are products). So we are not improving the lives of animals now; we are simply making the lives of animals in the future less horrible for us to look at. No animal will be thinking 'Phew! I'm glad I wasn't born

---

[68] http://www.baahaus.org/faqs.html Shows the life spans as follows: Beef Cattle 10-18 months, Chickens 6-8 weeks, Dairy Cows around 4 years, Lambs 3-5 months, Pigs 6-7 months, Turkeys 4-5 months. These figures are best guesses really, and we can confidently assert that animals live anywhere up to around 4/5 years as an economic matter.

10 years ago', just as no animals will be thinking 'This is bad, but it could be worse', as far as we know. And yet welfarism requires one of these to be true for it to be gaining ground.

Suffering of the sort experienced on any farm, where any animal is used as a piece of economic property, or in any slaughterhouse where animals are killed, is of a significant level. This is evolutionary common sense. Unless the cows are being sat in padded stalls, being fed their favourite foods, surrounded by their families, and killed in their sleep by pills ground up in their food, then of course their death is a major panic for them as they are a sentient, conscious organism. We're sentient in order to avoid death more efficiently, so it makes a lot of sense that we'd suffer greatly from not being able to avoid it, or thinking we are being trapped and led to it (indeed, many animals suffer such feelings from being trapped per se – as I mentioned already, they don't have the mechanisms to separate the two). Arguably that's the only reason suffering exists. In any case, it takes a huge level of irrational ignorance to pretend the animals are being killed painlessly, or to believe that welfare regulation is significantly better. 'Padding the water board', as Francione analogises,[69] will not make a difference to the animals whose suffering will still be significant, as well as the most horrendous experience of their short lives. An extra ten inches here, or a couple of trips outside, does nothing to alleviate 90% of the suffering an animal experiences – so we should be forgiven for asking if an animal who has never experienced worse would really be experiencing a better life of any sort in the new welfare 'enriched' conditions, let alone one worth campaigning for.

---

[69] Quoted from http://www.thescavenger.net/animals/the-abolitionist-approach-to-animal-rights-145.html

If we add these irrational conceptual mistakes that welfare regulation makes in its philosophising, to the fact that we now kill more non-human animals than ever before (consider industrial fishing especially, which dwarfs the 60 billion land animals killed yearly with an unconceivable figure of at least a trillion, as mentioned earlier), then it becomes clear that although we are arguably progressing in levels of civility and peace thanks to reason, violence isn't decreasing as we are finding ways to alleviate our consciences with more violence than ever before toward non-human individuals. Simply put, welfarism makes us feel better about violence toward animals – it is nothing but faith-based, misplaced compassion. Yet, ironically, if we were to extend reason to our treatment of animals, we would be much better off. So Pinker was right about that.

It was Edward Augustus Freeman who supposedly noted that, "The awful wrongs and sufferings forced upon the innocent, helpless, faithful animal race, form the blackest chapter in the whole world's history."[70] Technological advances now allow us to exploit animals with less appreciative qualities, not just the helpless faithful ones, but he still has a point. Animals, it seems, are the last moral taboo, and given the scarcity of rationalists who accept this, it is vital that they be considered heavily in any practical applications of rational morality.

---

[70] Freeman was a historian famed for his writing on the Norman Conquest; however, appeared to write little, to my knowledge, on animals. I include this quote with a note that it was supposedly stated by him, but as with so many historical quotes one can't be sure. It's better than not knowing who it was by and so just attributing it to Mark Twain on the basis that it sounded clever.

Chapter 5: Practical Ethics

Prelude

In one sense, a rational version of morality can appeal to a variety of current moral and social movements. By backing up claims made on behalf of individuals, or in opposing unfair, irrational systems that are impacting on a group of individuals' well-being. The main difference rational morality puts forth is that we have to change the way we think about ethics, with practical application being something of a potentially objective and logical nature, not a subjective personal taste or spiritual opinion. There are right and wrong answers to be gleaned – albeit of a very different type to classic moral realist ideas of 'moral facts' – and many of these answers already have social movements on their behalf, due to the rich variety of moral beliefs currently existing in the world. Similarly, many current moral movements do not make the slightest bit of sense as a moral matter. For example, the work of conservationists to capture animals, display them in zoos and force them to breed, as a way of helping the biological category of species rather than the sentient individuals who may suffer as a result of such action.

People often judge the value of ideas in relation to how well the idea sits with what they believe. So upon pointing out the practical application of rational morality, it is easy to worry that some may discard the theory altogether, simply by disagreeing with what it may require them to do. And hence at this point, I urge self-critical honesty and perspective. The great scientific advancements of our time were not made by embracing the norms, but were painstakingly rooted out in labs or in the field. These advancements themselves were made possible by pioneers of another time who were routinely oppressed by authorities that did not want truth to oppose their comfortable myths. Being morally and rationally consistent will not require this level of effort, but undoubtedly will require you do something, so a change in perspective is necessary. This requires action, or changes, perhaps, but hardly a great deal by historical comparison.

Practical application is what a rational morality is all about. The point of it is to show that we currently think erroneously about morality, and that our ethics should be evidence based. As a result, with classical forms of moral theory we see people talking in abstracts, and considering the most basic of ideas as constitutive of 'facts', or even supporting charities based on intuitive appeal to erroneous moral norms and values. However, with rational morality there is a real form of specific consequentialism. Rational morality is a realistic way to think about morality, built from science and rational consistency, and as such it doesn't take the view that morality is subjective and to be applied as to one's personal opinions, or one's knee-jerk reactions.

There will be areas where we can't honestly know what is best to do, as always. However, right now there is still an awful lot about which there is moral confusion, spreading from a growing misperception about moral relativism, which itself is most probably a misplaced extension of liberalism with regards to respecting one another (many believe that one can't claim that moral facts are real, so one must respect all opinions about it equally). As stated throughout, a rational version of morality shows this idea to be intellectually bankrupt, that there are many factual statements and actions we can make about reality, and that moral relativism itself makes claims about morality which aren't true.

To my mind, there are at least six main areas in society where morality is confused in the aforementioned way; on some of which opinion is currently entirely turned in the wrong direction. Please remember on reading the following five chapters that if what has been written so far at all appeals to you, then the idea of objective morality should also appeal. It is doubtful you will agree with all of these areas, but this is what morality is all about and where society has gone drastically wrong. There are right answers to be had and it is our responsibility to change our minds and amend our lifestyles accordingly. We ought to be rational, and adjustments to this may very well mean initial struggles to start being rational, rather than stubbornly decrying truth, facts and the relative nature of morality. Just like a good scientist doesn't cast the same theory over and over as correct in spite of evidence, a good person doesn't ignore moral logic in favour of short-term, comforting ignorance.

Remain critical and rational, but always open-minded to new evidence. And as I noted before, like we all wish to do, prioritise rational perspective over hard wired intuitions as much as possible. It's in moral quandaries where we see our own comfort challenged in the pursuit of fairness and truth, that we can experience a small fraction of what it was like to be Darwin discovering an unpleasant fact about why humans exist, or Galileo realising that he had evidence to contradict a 1,000-year-old tradition. Albeit only a small fraction, some might still say that discovering truth which disagrees with your own conventions is even more difficult than disagreeing with the powers in society. In this sense one can feel alive and liberated in freeing themselves from personal dogma, whilst owing a debt of gratitude to the great minds that allowed for a society where we can practice such freedom of opinion.

Nevertheless, just as dead-pan honesty might be required as to your current beliefs, a healthy dose of scepticism is encouraged. A scientific theory of morality is not about what I decide is right, any more than physics is about what any one physicist discovers. These chapters which follow are my thoughts as to the current rational state of things; thoughts that I hope are backed by strong arguments and evidence where required, but that I freely admit I may be wrong about. In essence, they mark nothing more than what would be brief investigations within moral science. Given science's wonderful ability to develop and improve, I am as sure that at least some of my thoughts will be wrong as I am that several of them will be controversial. But then admitting this is the beauty of science.

Rationality

I doubt the first section of practical application will come as any surprise: rationality. Yet this is not something that we, as human beings, have a proud history of accepting. Indeed, rational people are wrongly stereotyped as being cold, calculating machines, even though nothing could be further from the truth. Just like selfish acts are rationally thought-out, so are kind acts and compassionate acts. Explicit selfish acts tend to be thought-out by those who are misinterpreting rationality; people who only care about themselves, and act with a sentimental view of basic instinct rather than complex rational analysis. Whereas kind and compassionate acts are often the preserve of people who know they have enough security, and so are willing to impart some of it onto others. Not always, but often enough to allow a generalisation, I hope.

A rational, truthful theory of morality involves an acceptance that we ought to be rational. I explained this early on, as it's the crux of the theory. We are rational creatures, and as much as we may often find misplaced comfort in ignorance and hearsay, we are doomed/blessed (delete as appropriate) to consider decisions in a rational manner, whether we like it or not. However, there has yet to be any believable proof that any human being is, or ever has been, capable of making decisions on a non-rational basis. We sum up decisions in our minds, and act on the basis of our genes and our personalities, which are entirely constitutive of who we are. At no point do we act randomly or make choices we believe are irrational. We may *act* irrationally in every decision we make – by virtue of not seeing certain consequences or causes – but this doesn't mean the process of deciding how to act was ever random or non-rational in nature. At worst, we can be bad judges of external rationality, but we are never irrationally able in the sense that I have explained it.

Just as simply as the theory proposes rationality as the way our lives do function and the way they have to continue to do so whether we like it or not, falling in line with a consistent theory of morality (one which takes a fact-based position like other sciences do) involves starting to value and promote rationality as a societal matter as well as one of our natural capabilities. We will never be able to get away from our rational instincts, they underpin everything we do, and ignoring this in society is simply holding back our ability to find truth in traditionally non-scientific areas. Valuing rationality and everything it stands for – namely consistency – helps to foster a society where evidence, improvement, morality and respect are primary and where tradition, superstition, faith and prejudice are argued against. Of course there is no reason to value something simply because it is natural for us to do so, but as discussed at length earlier, rationalism isn't a choice like the other values we hold.

Indeed, we can describe emotions which we infer are generally morally significant (like kindness, compassion, evil and selfishness) by reference to rationality. After all, it is a rational process in our mind that determined we should act in this way. Thereby, rather than simply judging an action as kind, we can judge how rational it was as a factual matter. This does not mean saying 'Yes it was rational, as he decided to be kind and every decision is the result of a rational process', but rather 'Was it rational to exhibit kindness in that situation?' If it was in a situation during which one person had easily enough time or resources to exhibit kindness, and the other person was helped in some way by that decision – or indeed society was helped by it, as it fostered more of a respect for the emotion of kindness, which was needed as society was overtly selfish in nature – then it would seem to be rational. Alternatively, if a person starved because of being kind, whilst the recipient of the kindness already had more than enough resources, and society as a general rule was already being kind in nature, then it was not a rational choice to make. This is what we need to be wary of: absurd moral rules which preach irrational ideas. Rationality is not in the business of these sorts of abstract, universal principles, other than the universal principle of rationalism itself.

This individual explanation of circumstance is used to illustrate the point that kindness can be as irrational (and thereby immoral) as selfishness, and that selfishness can be as moral as kindness. The two are rationally formed and are perfectly rational responses to different situations. Most probably, the reason we deem kindness entirely positively and selfishness entirely negatively is due to the religious rules on it, which preach respect for a kind of martyrdom. A rational version of morality doesn't allow the self to be exploited at the expense of others, any more than vice versa.

Of course, these examples are only individual cases, and in a society with millions of people, where the inhabitants are not rational machines, it makes no sense to judge it unnecessary to have general moral rules about kindness or selfishness. As discussed at length earlier on, we need rules precisely because we are not rational machines. However, the explanation is necessary to show that there is no overarching or universal rule whereby kindness is positive and selfishness is negative, instead they both play important roles in rationality and in morality. Neither is the solution, nor is either the problem and hence this theory disagrees with the crux of many moral theories which judge at an aesthetic level that they are. Rationality is the solution.

This makes one other point clear: rationality is not just important after we attribute moral rules around kindness or respect, it is important in discovering those rules in the first place. It makes no sense to say, like Pinker does, that reason has extended empathy, which in turn has made society better for everyone (and so assuming we needed empathy first). Rather, what Pinker's important, practical analysis shows is that as we've become more rational, more empathy has been forthcoming as a result, and so society has gotten more civilised. Rationality is the increasing factor that has improved society. The old argument that rational decisions are cold and unforgiving is nonsense and holds no more water than the argument that spiritualists are better people than non-spiritualists.[71] We need to ditch these sorts of myths in order to progress into discovering real meaning. Accepting rationality and using reason is how we prove these myths wrong, and it's also how we progress with morality.

Atheism

As surely as morality requires rationality in order to be sound, our valuing of rationality can't be done in tandem with a valuation that belief in spite of evidence is something to be proud of.

Many claim that religious people can make rational decisions in other areas, so attacking the concept of faith is flawed. Of course they can, but this misses the point somewhat. We can all think rationally and only rationally in that sense, religion does nothing to change this in any individual. Thus the problem is not necessarily with our rational capabilities being diminished, but more with our rational intentions being reduced.

Consider the very worst example of religious dogmatism: extremist terrorism. A man wears a smile, happy in the knowledge that he and his family are going to a fulfilling afterlife, as he is about to fly a plane

---

[71] A good few studies, as mentioned earlier, show that spiritualists give more to charity, however this doesn't make them better people. Indeed it is the rational side of them, the side that believes that either they are gaining or will gain something from the giving, that compels them to give to charity a greater amount. The fact rationalists also give money to charity at all would be an argument that they are better people, as they believe no God or cosmic force is benefitting them by doing so. In truth, both are just as decent and as rational morality is taken on board we should see people being more rational and more charitable as a whole (though this doesn't necessarily mean giving money away, so much as making more charitable decisions), all be it more wary of poor charity ideas as also earlier mentioned. A reduction in the number of charities there are would also be a good, and hopefully predictable, sign.

full of innocent people into a tower also full of innocent people. If one looks at the psychological processes going on inside the man's head, it should become obvious that at no point is he making a decision which he believes to be irrational, or which is indeed formed irrationally. Given what he believes is true, what he is doing makes perfect sense. He believes God sets moral facts, that what he is doing is moral rather than immoral, and that he will be eternally rewarded for it. The problem is not that he reasons in an irrational manner, it's that he believes things with more assumptions than 'we ought to be rational'. These are faith-based, personal truths. There's no valuing of solid evidence there, and either he, or else the family or culture he lives in, has developed a respect for forming decisions in a dangerously irrational manner simply because they do not ask for evidence.

No one believes religion wholly consists of people willing to go to these extremes. However, it highlights exactly where the problem with religious thinking is. The problem is not that the rational capabilities of human beings in societies that value faith are reduced, it is more that the valuing of what constitutes facts and evidence is astoundingly irrational or non-existent, and that intentions to act and decide rational outcomes are reduced. The rational process is as fine in a religious person as in any other human being, the threat to public security comes with the idea that valuing faith, and forming beliefs without evidence, is a profoundly acceptable way to think and judge truth. Generally within society we understand that delusions are dangerous, and we should be consistent with this rational understanding no matter how culturally ingrained the delusion.[72] The arguments against this criticism, which are now forthcoming from many quarters, are many, but all seem lacking.

Not all religious people are terrorists

No, they certainly aren't, and no one should claim something so preposterously untrue. I grew up in a small community centred by a beautiful church and can attest to the fact that people weren't running around violently threatening nonbelievers nor disregarding the rights of others. But what does that prove? It shows that rationality, and its great pull on our minds, is enough to fight much faith-based dogmatism. As society becomes more secular (which itself shows we naturally tend toward rationality *anyway*), nonsensical laws such as blasphemy drop, as people no longer see it as important. Indeed, people rarely now hold witch trials or cat burnings either. Faith is diminishing in value in society, and so is irrationality, wholesale. Many of those people where I grew up might have been believers, but you can bet that when encountering each other on the streets and stopping for a chat, or helping one another out with some task, they were not doing so on pain of punishment from God if they didn't. They were mostly genuine and good people, and they believed in community. Had they been the types that needed the threat of divine punishment to keep them in line, it is difficult to imagine that they would have been quite so nice to one another.

---

[72] One will recognise the similarity to Harris' own arguments on this matter from *The End of Faith*, and many of his other works. His influence is neither hidden nor accidental, and his work on this subject, along with Dawkins, is truly pioneering.

This is an argument for further secularisation. Taking away the valuation of faith-based thinking is necessary in science if we want truth, as it reduces the ability for people to act unscientifically and prove things which aren't true. Similarly, once we view morality as an aspect of rational thinking, we also see a parallel need to reduce valuation of faith-based beliefs. Just as science wouldn't accept arguments attributed to God, society shouldn't accept them either. If morality is to be objective, it also needs to be rational.

Religion isn't irrational

So come the classic claims of pre-enlightenment society rearing their heads once again: *one cannot prove God doesn't exist, so it is not irrational to believe in him.* If one believes this is a good argument, one can't outwardly value science or rational arguments in the first place. Science never proves things 100% beyond doubt, truth simply doesn't work this way. There is always the possibility that a fact or a belief could be wrong upon discovery of new evidence. This doesn't make believing in things without evidence, or being unsure in spite of no evidence, a valid position. Certainly, making up statements with no evidence (God exists/the Easter bunny exists/gravity is just invisible jelly) does not make them true, or more true than ideas which haven't been said out loud. We must remember that *clarification on what nonsense entails doesn't make it any less nonsense.*

I couldn't scientifically claim gravity was 'a theory just as valid as invisible, strong jelly that pulls us to the Earth' because such an idea is hearsay with no evidence to back it up. I also couldn't rationally espouse racism as correct, believing whites to be supremely genetically different to people with other colours of skin. One doesn't have to be unsure about racism any more than one has to be unsure about invisible jelly or God. All are equally baseless in claim and neither could be considered justifiable positions, or indeed sound agnostic middle grounds, as there is definite favour for one side of the argument. Supporting agnosticism in these areas is decidedly irrational and inconsistent if we want to believe facts or truths exist at all.

The esteemed, late Professor Stephen Hawking explains the argument against religion in a way that sums it up nicely. He argues that physics leaves no room for God.[73] If there is no evidence for God, and there is no space for an explanation such as God in our understanding of the universe, then God is nothing more than a failed hypothesis. The inventor of the phrase 'New Atheism', Victor J. Stenger, has written extensively on this topic, and indeed he argues that given the religious hypothesis about God, we should have expected to see a variety of evidence for his existence, when in actual fact there is none. The book he wrote is called, unflinchingly and unsurprisingly, *God: The Failed Hypothesis*.

Arguments in favour of God dwell on the single idea that the burden of proof is on atheists, and yet they fail to note many other aspects of truth finding as Stenger has, or as I have briefly explained here.

Science can tell us how but not why, so religion/spirituality is fact finding of a different kind

Many people in modern society take this stance and admit facts of science as readily as they admit that religious/spiritual reasoning is needed

---

[73] *The Grand Design: New Answers to the Ultimate Questions of Life*. Stephen Hawking and Leonard Mlodinow.

to give us meaning, or explain why we are here. But how is this any different to the previous claim that religion isn't irrational?

Consider that I make up a new religion tomorrow as an experiment. I have no truth or experience to base it on, I simply start an online campaign to show that the meaning of our lives is to touch-type as fast as possible. There is a typing angel who watches over us, I claim, who created us all out of Times New Roman – a font which makes up our genetic code – and destined us to make keyboards in order to reach our hidden potential. Perhaps we could even find our 'inner letter' by doing this. Despite the fact I had no evidence and no experiential truth, would this be a relevant form of investigation into why we are here? Similarly, would our 'inner letter' be a sensible concept just because I had uttered the proposition regarding it? It bears repeating: *clarification on what nonsense entails doesn't make it any less nonsense.*

There is an unlimited amount of nonsense you could cobble together, and uttering one piece of it out loud doesn't suddenly make it truer than the infinite amount of nonsense that no one has ever uttered. When nonsense becomes culturally ingrained, it doesn't seem as silly as analogies like 'typing angels', but if you analyse it then there is no difference in evidence.

Science in fact has a perfectly good explanation of why we are here: we evolved. There was probably no creator at all, and we just happened into existence after millions of years of evolution, and many years before that of universal development which itself sparks from stellar events of what we believe was a phenomenon called the 'big bang'. An event in which space and time was created. Can we know how something can pop into existence from nothing? Not at the moment, as far as I can see, and physicists are beginning to argue that this is down to our misapprehending how time works (as time itself seems to have been invented when the big bang occurred, so there was nothing before; thus they argue that the question doesn't make sense, and our intuitions don't make sense). However unintuitive we find these arguments in physics, this doesn't mean that if I make up ideas, or take on board ideas from cultural definitions of God figures or 'experience', then it is likely to help in answering these questions.

In fact, that latter supposition – that 'experience' has a truth value of its own – is perhaps the most intuitive pull that this entire pro-religion argument has: the idea that science can measure and find truths in certain areas, but that to find truth on a meaningful level we need to look 'within ourselves' and find 'experiential truths' that science isn't capable of finding. Yet we have evolved from other primates (we still are primates, in fact), and at different points in history our ancestors have been in biological vehicles of various proportions going right back to single-celled organisms in primordial broth. Does it make sense to say that the meaning of an amoeba is for it to look inside of itself and find the 'why am I here?' Does it make sense that rats are missing out because they can only think from their own instincts, and can't decide not to eat today because they are contemplating how to find real meaning in their lives? Put next to the understanding of a scientific theory like evolution, 'why questions' like the above seem to miss the point of what rationality is.

All sentient individuals have some sort of rational mental mechanism helping them in their attempts to survive (not on the level of being able to create civilised science, or organised societies like we can, although species like ants appear to come close), yet none appear to have the ability to 'find truth from looking within'. Indeed, as an evolutionary matter, it makes sense to say that spiritual questions like this are misplaced rationality from a species that has grown so rationally capable, into such efficient, effective societies that it is has time to ask needless questions or create ways of trying to outwit its own rationality. Further irony, perhaps?

We can find meaning in an infinite number of ways that do not involve making spiritual and faith-based ideas up, and one wonders why it is that we are so desperate to escape the wonder of reality.

Spirituality can be explained

To finish off this section, which has argued throughout that rationality and atheism are necessary, morally important concepts, one has to take on board this final point which has been alluded to: spirituality, far from being a good method of finding meaning, is rationally explainable as a flawed hypothesis.

This is important, as no matter how many arguments are made against spirituality as a rational matter, there are still human beings who want to find meaning in it. They want to believe in the magical, or mythical, and a society which values faith (which our current society does) is one that gives people justification for continuing to listen to spiritual ideas in an act of unnecessary hope. Explaining spirituality for what it is may be the key in unlocking the rational ability of our society to discard faith and all the danger it entails.

So, consider the points I have made throughout this book so far. Human beings are unique in their rational capabilities. We can rationally attain our needs, we have evolved to be better and better equipped to do this, and are at the stage where we can consciously evolve our society in an instant (or at least in a few months or years) rather than having to wait many generations like in most examples of evolutionary biology in other species. We have thus attained a desire to search, continuously and entirely naturally, for ways of finding more truths; ways of seeking more and faster advancement.

Institutional science is an especially important and effective way of doing this, valuing as it does evidence, checks, the ability to repeat results, and the humility to admit it is wrong on points where evidence becomes available that shows said points were incorrect. I have argued that spirituality is the enemy of this, as it seeks to have us accept truths without evidence, and as Dawkins argues, to "be satisfied with not understanding the world".[74] However, I have also argued that we each, however much we try to avoid it, have an innate way of thinking which is based on rational decision-making. As such, spirituality can be defined as the erroneous, misplaced desire to be rational without a full understanding of what science and rationality involves.

And this is by no means a slight on religious or spiritual people, who I fully admit are striving for answers in ways they perceive to be rational. Some are also extremely capable in certain areas of science. Many scientists are often keen to note that they can't answer the 'big questions' and so take faith erroneously in ideas which are neither supported by evidence nor backed up in the way which a rational outlook would require. This shows us that many scientists *themselves* are often unfortunate products of a society in which faith is entirely misunderstood to be a valid way of finding rational answers. This further tells us that many scientists don't understand the importance of their methodology and are viewing it in immediately functional terms. This is no

---

[74] Quoted from the documentary entitled 'Enemies of Reason' originally aired on UK-based Channel 4.

great shock. Wanting to answer a 'why are we here?' type question is incredibly compelling, and difficult to see as the nonsensical question it is for most people. It is enlightening, yet difficult, to realise that the very question assumes the meaning that it is meant to be asking about, and thus is nothing more than illogical hyperbole. This brings us to the final point in this chapter.

Faith is a problem

The problem is not people comforting themselves near death with a belief in an afterlife, or people looking to the teachings of Jesus for moral guidance. Though this latter point may be mistaken, as the Christian author CS Lewis noted, "You can shut him up for a fool, you can spit at him and kill him as a demon, or you can fall at his feet and call him Lord and God. But let us not come with any patronizing nonsense about his being a great moral teacher. He has not left that open to us."[75] Neither is the problem of scientists not knowing the answers to what we think are the 'big questions', which might simply be the questions of a species who don't understand the nature of what answers are meant to be, or how to tell an important question from one which assumes a concept which can't possibly exist. The moral problem is that we aren't raised or educated to value rationality.

The fact we see answers based around nothing but a faith, or the attitude of having faith as a positive, moral way of reasoning, shows we haven't understood what faith is. We are human beings; individuals evolved from a variety of other organisms, but still just organisms. No doubt consciousness causes us problems in science, as it asks difficult questions akin to the other great scientific investigations in history. But

---

[75] *Mere Christianity*. C.S. Lewis.

the fact that we can rationalise things in a way that's unique in the animal kingdom does not make us special, and the fact that we are so efficient that we have time on our hands does not mean that questions we posit demand answers that science and rationality cannot provide. Perhaps, as I've shown, the questions themselves only make sense as a grammatical matter; to ask for the 'meaning' of life might be no more sensible than asking for the 'meaning' of keyboards. We invented grammatical rules and they work well most of the time but they do not necessarily guarantee that a question makes sense as a logical matter.

Faith asks people not only to be satisfied with not understanding (thus asking them to throw their support behind fairy tales), but it also asks people to forgo decisions that are made with evidence and reason in relation to reality, for those that are made through the same rational mental processes but with no such evidence or reasoning. What's worse is that we don't just use faith to answer personal questions that reason cannot yet answer, or to answer questions that themselves don't make sense, we also employ faith in politics, sometimes in science, and most problematically in judging whether acts are moral or immoral. Faith is simply not capable in areas like these, where objective facts are important. And furthermore, it is credible to note that a society that stands for faith at all, valuing as it does the ideas which oppose rationality, will cultivate a society that feels no need for rational consistency. This doesn't just mean we see blunted science, with many not interested in answers, but we also see a society with a stagnating moral compass in which faith and reason are equal, and thus where morality is a subject of personal tastes rather than objective moral consequences. Faith in one's own opinions, however formed, is not likely to lead to courageous and correct moral truths.

What this does *not* mean, as a practical matter, is that we should discriminate against those with religious views or incite violence. Being rational is about being fair to people. However, we need to begin challenging the value of faith wherever it occurs: in people, in institutions and in society as a whole. It's no longer something we can ignore, and with the threat of biological and nuclear weapons of mass destruction, along with an animal population of trillions being decimated each year, faith needs to be cast away from serious discussion for the same reason that prejudice is currently being erased. What we need more than anything is people looking to evidence and science for answers, rather than pitting their gods or imaginary facts against one another. The latter could destroy the world, as it isn't open to rational, sensible, evidence-based discussion like science is; proponents cannot be proved wrong and so can take things to an extreme, fatal level of disagreement. Similarly, we can no longer pretend faith is the preserve of gentle people when we live in a society where religious terrorism has killed thousands in the last few years alone, and where religion is fighting back for its place in government across the world. The stand needs to be of rationality against *all* faith; of the secular against the religious; of good ideas against bad ideas.

Chapter 6: Animal Ethics

The premise of a rational theory of morality that was set up earlier in the book, and which guided us with three principles – of freedom, protection of interests and fairness – has so far primarily been talked about in relation to humans. As animals are unable to consent to such a cooperative theory of morality, it seems of little importance to involve them in most of our concerns. However, I believe that means we owe them only one right – a sentiment taken from animal rights theory – of the right not to be used or treated as property. They cannot thrive in human society like we can, they cannot become participants in any social contracts we create, and as such it is pointless to consider them within the principle. Similarly, to create blanket rights to life for other animals would, I believe, deter from the ability for us to flourish. But their sentience argues that, in return for not having to grant them further protections we should leave them alone wherever reasonably possible. The following chapter makes that case and explores the theory of animal ethics from a rational perspective.

Sentience

Almost all societies have come a long way from the influential Cartesian, flawed understanding of animals as unfeeling machines.[76] Such is further recognition of the useful role science plays in society, that far from viewing animals as machines, or as soulless individuals to be looked down upon, most of us now view animals for what they are: sentient individuals at various places in an evolutionary tree.

Just as humans evolved from singular celled organisms, every animal alive today is also the product of millions of years of rich evolutionary history; history which has created such an array of sentient individuals, that it would take more than anyone's lifetime to understand even the basic differences of each different species.

As far as morality is concerned, though, we need not be directly concerned with single-celled organisms, or trees, or plants. We need only concern ourselves with sentient individuals. Throughout I make

---

[76] *Discourse on the Method.* Descartes, R. 1637.
It has been bought to my attention that the Philosopher John Cottingham has criticised and argued against this widely regarded view that Descartes held animals as nothing more than unfeeling machines. Cottingham has written a paper entitled *'A Brute to the Brutes?': Descartes' Treatment of Animals* in which he examines Descartes writings on this matter, and argues that although he did believe them to be machines, he may well have regarded them as being sentient to some degree. A high amount of scepticism exists within this piece, and it is unlikely to ever be backed up hard evidence either way. For the purposes of my using Descartes' widely attributed view, it matters little whether Descartes actually believed it or not; the view itself was influential, and descriptive of an 'unfeeling' toward animals which describes more accurately the historical context of the human view of other animals as opposed to the more sympathetic view we hold today. We can happily call this 'unfeeling' perspective a Cartesian influenced view, either way, as it was influenced and widely attributed to Descartes.

reference to this, and here seems as good a reason as any to explain it (not that it should require much explanation).

To be a subject of moral respect, one has to be able to experience one's life. To our best scientific understanding, trees are 'unfeeling machines' by virtue of being organisms that act on non-conscious process, grow and naturally respond to stimuli in all manner of ways. Like rocks, they have no nervous system, nothing central that is conscious and experiences what is happening to them or around them.

Biology and physics offer us the categories of physical vs non-physical, organic vs non-organic, or even inanimate vs animated. But the most important moral distinction we can draw appears to be between the conscious and the unconscious. We know (as far as we can know) that we are conscious. We can feel pain, we can experience contentment to some degree and we are *subjects of our own lives*, as the American philosopher Tom Regan theorised.[77] We know that this isn't because we are organic and grow or respond to stimuli (like any organism can), but rather because of our central nervous system which evolves *after* the ability to respond to stimuli does. Nerves transmit stimuli which cause pain; a brain experiences the pain and takes the pain on board to tell the nerve to stop experiencing that pain, and thus the process of this emotion acts as a negative feeling to the person experiencing it. In being subjects of lives, rather than organic machines, we experience this as conscious individuals. There is something to experience the reaction (me), rather than just the action happening by itself. That's a basic scientific description of sentience at work. To be sceptical of sentience itself seems more paranoid than sceptical, and indeed we see further evidence and agreement about sentience as a

---

[77] *The Case for Animal Rights*. Tom Regan, 1983.

scientific matter every year.[78] This is the norm within the scientific community, and within Western society.

Upon the scientific realisation that experiencing life is not related to organisms so much as to consciousness (of which concepts like a central nervous system are a marker for, as they transmit messages for a central brain to create a 'sensing' of it), our understanding of evolution comes in handy. We know we evolved from other primate species, and so when we look at primates and see a similar biological make-up, in many ways it makes sense to start connecting the dots and noting that there are individuals that are not human that are probably sentient. Indeed it is to advance a faith-based position to state that consciousness appears only once a species has evolved into the human species. The biological similarities and existence of a nervous system in so many other individuals would make such a claim invalid. Simple observation of the facts makes it untenable, and as Voltaire put it many years ago, "People must have renounced, it seems to me, all natural intelligence to dare to advance that animals are but animated machines...It would be very strange that they should express so well what they could not feel."[79]

The recognition that animals appear to experience emotions, coupled with our best scientific knowledge of how sentience is marked in our own species, make it a steadfast fact that at least some animals are sentient. As well as humans and other primates, the group of sentient animals must also include animals with similar biological consistency

---

[78] http://fcmconference.org/ This, the Francis Crick Memorial Conference 2012, was the latest development in non-human consciousness, in which a declaration was signed by scientists as renowned as Stephen Hawking in order to fully attest to the idea that non-human consciousness exists.
[79] *Traité sur la Tolérance*. Voltaire, 1763

and physical traits such as cows, pigs, dogs, geese, chickens, birds, many fish, giraffes…the list is almost endless, and we can't know for sure where it stops (for instance some classifications of animals, like sponges, actually appear to be non-sentient, so perhaps we also shouldn't rule out the idea that some non-animal organisms can be sentient).

However, we can be fairly sure that most, if not all, animals we generally use in industry and otherwise affect in society are sentient. Moreover, it doesn't hurt to be careful. Just as we wouldn't remove life-saving medication in any normal situation where we weren't sure a human was still a subject of life, or whether he or she had died and so was no longer sentient, we also shouldn't allow ourselves to exploit an individual of another species when we genuinely aren't sure of their sentience.[80] Logical extensions of any rational version of morality would stretch to non-human animals, perhaps even as far as some insects like bees.

We can therefore be reasonably rationally assured that many animals are sentient, but why is sentience of moral importance? Why rationally discard those organisms or physical objects that aren't sentient? Why not extend morality to everything? Well, morality is about well-being. Just as the umbrella term of 'health' makes no sense when applied to rocks or kettles or flag poles, morality doesn't either. We can show morality to be intensely rational, and extend morality to be a

---

[80] Of course such a principle, in human or nonhuman relations, could be sacrificed if it were the case that one's life was threatened. For instance, in the event of a plane crash on a remote island it wouldn't necessarily be irrational to kill and eat a rabbit for continued survival if it were all the nourishment that was available, just as it wouldn't be irrational to eat a fellow passenger if he was all that was available.

consistent move, but we can't show rational reason for extending it to non-sentient organisms or objects as there is no subject of a life in them with which to experience any change in moral treatment. Nothing conscious to experience the actions. Morality relates only to sentient organisms (or sentient non-organisms, even), for the same reason that biology relates to organic organisms, or geology relates to physical facts and forces.

What is meant by this is not the naturalistic argument – that morality relates only to organisms because it always has, and is defined to do as such. It is rather the argument that I – nor anyone else – can fathom what a morality aimed at non-sentient items would look like, as it's a logical paradox. We can reference non-sentient items as useful to the well-being of conscious individuals, but it doesn't make any logical sense to talk about the well-being of something which physically exists but does not consciously experience life itself. We can ponder – as Thomas Nagel did – what it is like to be a bat, only as there appears to be something that it is like to be a bat. In other words, a bat appears to experience life, so we can at least ponder their sentience; the ability to feel what happens around or to them. Whereas non-sentients such as grass or rocks lack anything to which morality could relate, in the same way that cement mixers lack anything that food refrigeration can relate.

So the point stands that this area of discussion, that non-human animals can be subjects deserving of ethical consideration, should affect us a great deal. As I earlier noted, we can be fairly sure that most of the animals we use in human industry are sentient, amounting to tens of billions of land animals every year and potentially over a trillion aquatic creatures.[81]

Welfarism

It felt odd writing that last chapter, as one wonders if most readers would have needed it. We live in a society where even TV chefs and exploitative tabloid newspapers champion the causes of different non-human animals, so why would I think the reader needed to be encouraged to see that animals are sentient, like us? Consider it more of an academic foundation to be built upon.

The TV chefs and tabloid media are actually remarkably good markers of how society feels: transmitting, as they do, the 'safe' norms and values of society, so they don't disintegrate their popularity by alienating their audience. Western society, almost as a whole, views animals as individuals with interests. As such it shocks us all to see chickens crammed ten to a tiny cage, or dogs abused by immature or violent owners. Our championing and support of causes related to opposing these sorts of actions speaks well of our intentions.

However, the 'welfarism' from which these campaigns spring (that aim to improve our treatment of animals) is currently counter-productive at best and absolutely irrational at worst. In chapter 4 I discussed the issue, and the work of Professor Francione who has shown the flaw

---

[81] The Food and Agriculture Organization of the United Nations is the generally used source for statistics on land animals (noting 56 billion land animals per year in 2003), whilst the figures on sea animals is much more difficult to gauge as catches in the oceans are often measured in tons rather than numbers of individual animals. The only known source I could find was as follows (estimating the number of fish as in the region of 1-2 trillion): http://www.fishcount.org.uk/published/standard/fishcountfullrptSR.pdf)

in its legal process. Welfarism does little for animals but make their exploitation more efficient. As a philosophical matter, welfarism appears to improve little for animals. This is due to Francione's economic argument that the costs of significant improvement couldn't be taken on board in welfarist campaigns, and because the reasoning behind supposed improvements assumes animals have human feelings that their situation could be 'better or worse'; psychological traits which they are incredibly unlikely to hold. The success of welfarism is both economically unlikely and psychologically impossible.

Indeed, I characterised Pinker's own analysis of welfarism's great improvements for animals as incorrect because although we are arguably progressing in levels of civility and peace thanks to reason, violence isn't decreasing as we are finding ways to alleviate our consciences with more violence than ever before, just in the direction of non-human individuals. This is extremely important. Rational morality acknowledges that as we become more rational, society will morally improve. Pinker in a roundabout way agrees, stating as he has that "there has never been a better time to be a potential victim".[82] However, animal use is one of the ways in which we trick ourselves into seeing rational improvement, when in fact we are actually just making irrational claims. Not least because we don't like the idea of challenging ourselves to change anything significant about our lifestyles. This 'speciesism' is so ingrained in our society that even Pinker's analysis in *Better Angels of our Nature*, which in my mind is one of the greatest academic achievements of the 21st century so far, fails to spot its effect in blunting the good intentions of welfarism.

---

[82] Taken from his Ted talk, http://www.youtube.com/watch?v=ramB-FRt1Uzk. This idea is also alluded to in Pinker, 2011.

Anti-speciesism – and ethical veganism – has to be the moral baseline

Rationalists, like everyone else, are desperate not to have to look inward on any subject, and whilst I imagine stating atheism as a moral imperative will still raise a few eyebrows, it is the claim of anti-speciesism which I suspect will bring out the faith-based fear in otherwise rational people. Yet anti-speciesism makes perfect sense: we are not talking about creating a society that sees humans and animals as equally able, it is an entirely different 'ism' in this sense. We simply need to inject rationality to any situations where we indulge prejudice based on species. Anti-speciesism arguably only requires ethical veganism on a personal level, which is the practice of eliminating animal products (as far as is possible) from one's diet and lifestyle. No cuddling cows, no joining PETA, and no giving dogs a right to vote. And certainly no throwing red paint over people. Just *rational veganism*, which I am well aware might be two words that have rarely deserved to be read in tandem before. But why do I think we need to go this far, rather than settle with a better form of welfarism?

Welfarism is a hit or miss system of trying to look out for animal interests. Before we even get to the mammoth practical problems with trying to garner rights for individuals who are legally and socially seen as property (as explained in chapter 4), there is one basic irrational flaw in welfarism: the assumption that animals are our products to be used in the first place. We certainly could back animal use on the same grounds that we can back our belief in God. Perhaps even more so, because we eat animals in our meals every day, we wear them on our bodies, we even rub their excretions into our skin. Animal use is perhaps more imbedded into our being than religion is, and as such, the mountain path away from animal use is intertwined with the one of fighting other types of dogma. It takes an honest person to point out that animal use is entirely tradition-based, and not at all rational, and that eliminating animal use from our lives is not just rationally preferable, it is the very baseline of rational morality (given the potential billions of otherwise victims). I stated rational morality wasn't a game of numbers in terms of formulae and equations, but when we are justifying the deaths of trillions of animals every year based purely on our will to continue our traditions and habits, the numbers speak for themselves.

It is easy to ignore such a point on the grounds that vegans are traditionally spiritually inclined, tie-dye and sandal wearers, with a penchant for peace signs instead of progress. However, those of us who have cast out ideas about God, and created entire movements opposing theism and encouraging skepticism about the paranormal, are better placed than most to see through the social stigma. We are also more rationally able to see the problems with the industry approved system of welfarism.

I won't explain the hideous uses of animals we indulge ourselves in yearly, and neither will I go into them. You can find the horrific pictures and videos of all types of animal use in various places – from books and papers, to news bulletins and YouTube – so I've no need to waste your time here. If one wants to make claims that the supposedly humane use of cows, pigs, chickens, fish, etc., anywhere on Earth justifies our choosing meat, dairy, eggs or leather, rather than something non-animal-based when shopping, then let's not delude ourselves. No one reading this is naïve enough to think this is a sound argument, or

125

one which their neutral rationality is pointing to; we use animals primarily out of taste or convenience, and it is very difficult to rationally justify any kind of death or suffering (however humane we believe them to be) by holding our tastes on a pedestal. Rather, our use of animals is entirely needless. There's little, if anything, we need to use them for, and as decent, rational people it's time we really started to think decently and rationally. There is probably no God, and there's definitely no reason we can't walk past the butcher's section in the supermarket. If the effort of a little thought and care by the consumer is not morally outweighed by the immense suffering and eventual early deaths of billions of entirely sentient individuals every year, then we simply are not looking at the evidence in the right way. There is no moral fact as solid as this one, as far as I can see. It may well be time to create a movement for *rational anti-speciesism* or *rational veganism*.

Deleting the 'moral contract' thesis

There's one very intuitive criticism of stating anti-speciesism as a moral baseline. I have stated throughout that morality is rational as it serves us well. We ought to be rational, as being rational not only means we get truth rather than personal opinion (as irrationality 'fudges' results), but as a practical matter it naturally asks us to go and create a better world for everyone by virtue of not allowing as many risks. You might be one of the victims of a world where victims are commonplace: reducing the number of victims, by improving everyone's security, theoretically reduces the risk of you being one. A rational morality includes altruism that thus happens to be self-serving as well as entirely rational and scientific. This is, I believe, one of the great practical strengths.

This undoubtedly brings up an important issue. Animals are not party to respecting this morality and cannot intellectually follow moral laws, so why should they be included at all? There appears to be no benefit to us.

This criticism is intuitive because it views morality as a selfish, rational tool; perhaps one that I have exploited by stating the practical benefits of the theory. However, as I've explained, the pragmatics are not the primary thing. Once we accept morality as a rational discipline, like we accept physics as a rational discipline for understanding and improving our world, then it becomes a case of making it rational. We don't 'fudge' the results in physics and plump for answers simply because they serve us well,[83] so why would we fudge the results in morality just because it serves us better? That's not morality, that's just exercising selfish will.

Moral science, once accepted as a discipline of rationality like the others (physics, maths, biology, etc.), which is the only way we can usefully accept it, becomes constitutive of the same rules. If one area is useful for advancing our world then it becomes a case of rationality. The same goes for them all equally, else we are doing precisely what the moral relativist does, in judging morality to be subjective and useful only as a pragmatic matter, or what the spiritualist does in judging

---

[83] Of course, one might argue we do fudge results in physics to some degree, by only exploring those fields which are useful to us to explore. My point with the analogy, though, is that we don't just change the figures; we couldn't else we would shoot ourselves in the foot as our theories wouldn't work. Physics by definition cannot generally fudge results. However, if there were examples where physicists could just make up ideas, it would certainly be looked down upon. Indeed those who try to fudge quantum mechanics results by twisting them to seemingly prove spiritual positions could be said to be fudging results. Such 'woo' is looked down upon by physicists and seen to be devaluing the subject, rather than being given any sort of truth value.

truths where there is no evidence. It may be true that morality evolved as a sort of moral contract, but that doesn't mean we must persist with it as such, for the same reason that if physics developed as a way of worshipping and understanding God's creation, it doesn't have to continue as such.

However, there is a practical relevance; one that has been with us for many years. Kant explained the necessity to be kind to animals in purely anthropocentric terms. He didn't believe animals themselves had interests, as he didn't view them as rational.[84] He believed that we should be kind to animals as it fosters respect to each other as humans. Indeed, some modern-day studies back this up, and show that violent criminals often have a history of abusing animals.[85] As the psychologist Bradley Millar is credited for saying, "Teaching a child not to step on a caterpillar is as valuable to the child as it is to the caterpillar."[86] In essence, what is being gotten at is the idea that animals are sentient individuals: they can be caused pain, and they can even show it in remarkably understandable ways to us humans. Teaching people to ignore this expression of pain and to see it as a necessary part of their own life is an astoundingly easy way to make people numb to the moral pull which sentience naturally has on us. It assists people in ignoring it in humans and in ignoring our rational ability to perceive it. This doesn't seem too far off as an idea, and as much as we need more evidence to put this point into practice, it must still give hope that even

---

[84] *The Metaphysics of Morals*, Immanuel Kant, 1797.
[85] https://www.ncjrs.gov/pdffiles1/ojjdp/188677.pdf
[86] This is another credit, but unsure of the source validity. In any case, it once again is the proposition I want to allude to rather than using the source as proof, and so I don't hesitate in using it.

the most selfish among us will respect the ideal of anti-speciesism, as well as the more scientific or rational among us.

Society currently tries to evade this potential problem by hiding away slaughterhouses and employing lower-class individuals to be the ones causing the suffering on our behalf. We even hide the realities of farming from our children with the same ferocity that we hide violent movies, or the details of immoral murders. But are we really hidden from it, and can we ever be? It seems to me that we naturally want to know where our food comes from and it also seems illiberal for governments to try to hide this for our own good, as well as being an instance of irrationally fudging results. Furthermore, it seems to breed faith-based irrational thinking to try to teach children that they must respect other people by virtue of their sentience and ability to experience life, but that they can ignore sentient subjects of a life in other biological categories: this is arbitrary rule setting of the type which we abhor when done in science, or in other areas of life. And I'm not sure it could ever be a good idea in a rational version of morality – again, failing to plan for this kind of problem is planning to fail.

The practical aspects of animal use, however briefly considered, may be significant. We seem to naturally react to the sentience of others (we evolved as social creatures, so it would be strange that we wouldn't), and teaching people that it isn't sentience but rather the category of 'being human' that should be respected, appears to be missing something rather important.[87] But in any case, we have to remember that science isn't about practicalities; they are nice to have, but the goal is consistency.

Removing prejudice

Racism, sexism, homophobia, there are many forms of prejudice still strong in the world. Speciesism is one of a different type but is prejudice in kind all the same. Just as it's irrational to discriminate arbitrarily based on race or sex, it is irrational to discriminate arbitrarily based on species. Just as we don't want to teach our kids to think in terms of justifying irrational prejudice, we adults shouldn't think in those terms either. Progression involves rooting out these kinds of opinions.

Speciesism looks a lot different to known, accepted prejudices because it involves non-humans. Normal claims of prejudice are often invoked upon the violation of human rights, like to not be given a vote or to be denied freedom to travel to certain areas. We've no need to put animals into this kind of legal framework. We possibly need just give them one right, as Francione suggests, the right not to be used as property. By doing this we avoid the difficult if not impossible talk about

---

[87] It is not just society that preaches that human beings are the markers of respect, even the human rights campaign group Amnesty International for many years hosted the slogan 'Protect the Human'. For a long time I've seen problems with this slogan, judging as it does that same 'independent moral fact' theory that humans 'just are' what is important to look after. I have never been comfortable with rules without understanding or evidence, and my experiences of amnesty volunteers who could not grasp why I am vegan, or the reasons for 'sentience' rather than 'human' being the marker of moral interests, were probably perhaps the earliest catalysts for the theory of rational morality. It is fitting they should be alluded to at some point, and fitting also that it be mentioned they do an awful lot of good work for human beings; work which I mostly do not oppose, of course.

manslaughter of insects when we go running on grassy fields, and we also avoid odd ideas like having to make other animals people in the same way humans are seen (useful if not only because it would be very difficult to discourage the apathy of dogs in general electoral votes).

A right not to be used as property is thus common sense; a rational recognition that a sentient individual is not a piece of property and thus has interests. Thereby we shouldn't be attributing ownership over them in the first place. This means nothing more than leaving them alone most of the time. We can't pretend we know what they want, or even how they feel in any profound manner, but we can know that they experience suffering and would be better off without it. Allowing them a right not to be used as property is a simple legal safeguard against the use of animals in human industry, or in any behaviour which would attempt to use them as a target of human exploitation. This is simple, rational anti-speciesism at work. As a personal matter it involves the recognition of the importance of being a dietary (at least) vegan, and the abstention from consuming animal products oneself. Perhaps also the adopting of the victims of our current pet or farming systems. In many years (undoubtedly not in our lifetimes), one would like to see the legal part of the theory become relevant also.

Mountaineering the academic Alps

Advocating anything involving veganism in the current academic climate might seem analogous to advocating evolution in the time of Darwin. And yet, the basis is there for all to see. Dawkins spoke of the irrational nature of speciesism way back in the 70s in *The Selfish Gene*, and Harris' pioneering ideas in *The Moral Landscape* note that it is the well-being of *sentient individuals* and not just humans that matter. The

131

most rational conclusion is to discard this irrational idea that animals are naturally our property in the first place, for the same reason that young children are no longer considered property.

Nevertheless, one feels compelled to lay myths out on the table here, to stop them where they start. The following are all irrational ways to palm off the moral obligation that veganism involves. A good dose of well-natured skepticism is required.

Veganism is not healthy, natural or convenient

There exist millions of vegans in the world, and indeed many cultures throughout history have forgone meat regularly, whilst a reliance on eggs and dairy is about as unnatural as any food stuff one could think of; factory processed foods certainly look a lot better when you consider the factories for eggs and milk are the innards of farmyard animals. The Western world's influence is the factor which has recently pushed countries like India and China, in particular, away from largely plant-based diets.[88] Vegan diets (though not known as 'vegan' in any area until the 1950s when Donald Watson coined the term) have probably always existed somewhere, and they have been able to as there exists no nutrient that one can only gain from animal products. It is a distinct bias from our own cultures that allows us to see the vast importance of foods like green vegetables, without also seeing that foods like meat and dairy do not contain anything particularly unique or special. And indeed, it is a profound (and in some sense understandable, up to now) ignorance that stops us from obtaining the evidence that unveils the truth.

---

[88] *Resisting the Globalization of Speciesism: Vegan Abolitionism as a Site for Consumer-Based Social Change.* Wrenn, C. L. 2011.

Calcium exists in much higher proportions from sources like green vegetables or even soya beans than it does in dairy. 'Protein deficiency' is something one could only realistically suffer from whilst starving to death (one could eat only potatoes and not be deficient in protein). Iron, omega 3 and iodine can all be catered for in abundance (despite advertisements and schemes run from the animal industry stating the opposite). The mysterious vitamin B12 (of which theories suggest we either evolved a need for by gaining its advantages via eating unwashed plant foods or feasting on the liver of some animals) can be created in reliable sources in labs and fortified into almost anything we eat. Whilst vitamin D, a nutrient that most of us don't get enough of in any diet (including on vegan diets), is easily catered for vegans and non-vegans alike via vegan supplements, instead of the non-vegan supplements that most people in countries like the UK (with its limited months of quality sunlight) should be taking.

Indeed, one wonders whether the claim of veganism being unhealthy is really believed at all. People eating nothing but meat will likely be some way more nutritionally deficient than those eating nothing but plants – however ill-informed they are – yet we don't see the same prejudice toward people with barbeque addictions as we do to vegans.

More importantly, people tend to believe that veganism is either unnatural or inconvenient – two claims which are more believable. Yet, unnatural? As a claim from a species that has flown to the moon, created towering buildings in super cities, and managed to both trawl the depths of the deepest oceans and soar to the highest points in the atmosphere, one wonders whether we really should judge the usefulness of an action by its relation to being natural. While on the other hand,

133

everything we can do is natural as we are animals, and some things which are entirely natural in other species (like infanticide and the killing of sexual partners) or were common in early versions our own species (like rape or genocide) are not judged moral by their value of being natural. Nature does not judge morality well, and can only ever be arbitrary in moral claims. Hence, we often value 'being natural' well below the value of 'being immoral', so such an argument should have little say on the subject of veganism.

Inconvenient, then? One can't argue with that as veganism is certainly more inconvenient at current than non-veganism. And yet one could say the same thing about many social injustices in the past. It was once much easier to partake in all kinds of things than to oppose them (the oppression of women in Europe throughout history and the fascism of Nazi Germany in the 1930s to name but two). And yet many did oppose them, and we like to think we still would. Furthermore, choosing to ignore buying products that have been made via chaining animals up or killing them, is hardly going to require the same bravery as opposing a Nazi state or a patriarchal Tudor monarch (either of which could easily result in your murder). A bit of perspective wouldn't go amiss. If moral progress didn't involve changing lifestyles or opinions to some degree, then it wouldn't be moral progress in the first place. For most of us, we are talking about buying something different in a shop or cooking something different in our homes. As moral choices go, this is as easy as they come.

It seems accurate to label our inability to see veganism as relatively easy to itself be a product of extremely irrational thinking. It's inconvenient, occasionally, to choose to be vegan only because more people haven't done it. Whether we like it or not we live in a capitalist society, where supply changes (based on the demand) in an effort to make as much money as possible. If people demanded vegan products and refused to buy animal products, supply would change rapidly. And that is exactly what is happening in the UK right now. I went vegan around 12 years ago, and at that time I made up my junk food (yes, I was a student at the time) from powdered boxes to replace my ordinary non-vegan meals. Now a visit to just one supermarket will throw up dozens of burgers, sausages, chicken, pâtés and all manner of other vegan alternatives. Not to mention that large swathes of the stores – these things called vegetables, fruits, nuts, etc. – were already vegan. Vegan products have been one of the fastest growing food trends in the country for several years running, because people started demanding them instead of welfare-raised versions of animal products. Change is happening.

Flexitarianism and Welfarism: the utilitarian position strikes again

Flexitarianism refers to the kinds of positions taken by the likes of the philosopher Peter Singer when referring to animal use. A flexitarian doesn't see veganism as the ideal, but rather as one of many ways to reduce animal suffering. As such, veganism may be discarded in a pragmatic manner, such as when at a restaurant and served cheese accidentally, or for the pleasure of purposefully eating steak occasionally. It may make much more sense for someone like Singer to just eat the cheese or steak, contributing to a greater overall happiness at the dinner table, so as to make veganism seem more pleasant or likeable.

Again, we see the fallacy of shallow pragmatism here. This won't just make the vegan in question seem pleasant and easy, it will also make them seem inconsistent,[89] and will make veganism seem like an unimportant decision to be waded in and out of as one wishes and finds easy to do; pushing those same norms about morality being personal and taste-based which we have identified is the problem, not the solution.

Furthermore, social movements work like snowballs. The movement against animal use can only do the same: people will reject animal use or accept it. Positions like flexitarianism ('veganism occasionally'), or even like welfarism itself ('animal use is okay'), take the focus away from what is right (anti-speciesism) and make it look instead like there are several right answers. Each 'right answer' becomes equally valid as a personal choice, and thus the perceived easiest ones will flourish, and the perceived hardest ones will naturally be left to stagnate. Similarly, if these are all right answers, why can't most people reason that their own answer of 'do nothing, but act concerned in social situations' as equally right? Society has already changed opinion from 'animals have no sentience' to 'animals deserve some interests', and yet we appear to exploit more animals now than ever before. Even with a growing world population, the figure is still significant enough that this is still a definite sign of evidence against ideas like flexitarianism. If caring attitudes were enough, why aren't we doing better?

Veganism is the rational choice with regards to animal ethics, and yet it will always look harder than 'veganism when I feel like it' or 'non-

---

[89] All-or-Nothing Games in the Civil Rights Movement. Social Science Information 30: 677-697. Chong, D. 1991. Chong shows that collective "goods" can be destroyed by a single compromise, which is very similar to the situation with veganism. Whilst Chong is focusing on protesting events in the civil rights movement, it is easy to draw similarities to the vegan education cause, where 'defectors' like Singer can cause huge problems for many important aspects of vegan education.

veganism but occasionally buy animal products with a nicer looking label' or more appropriately 'do nothing but feign concern'. The movement against animal use can only progress like any other social movement in history, picking up speed as it gathers momentum by getting more people on side. And yet, what the likes of Singer's position does is to take support away from the growing snowball, providing justification for not joining the movement at all. Flexitarianism and welfarism provide the same effect to anti-speciesism that spirituality and agnosticism do to anti-theism.

Like other forms of utilitarian theory, flexitarianism is entirely irrational when considered as a pragmatic or scientific matter. It makes as much sense as partial opposition to rape, or occasional opposition to racism, and it's only because these things are against the law that flexitarianism isn't judged with the same intensity. If Singer were to suggest flexitarianism with respect to eating farmed humans (after all, he claims humans and animals are equal in suffering) one would assume the morally untenable position he advocates would be easier for most to oppose.

All animal ethics helps? The Welfarism flaw

As someone who has been involved in animal ethics for many years, more of my time has been spent on explaining why that statement in the subtitle doesn't make sense than anything else. There is a mistaken assumption that as humans become kinder, everything gets better; thus all animal ethics is positive in net effect by pushing the interests of animals, and thereby pushing us to be more empathetic.

There is intuitive appeal to this widely believed statement. Over time, as we have grown more rational, we have undoubtedly become kinder and less harsh with each other and so in turn, society is now a better place to live. Pinker argues this with the strongest analysis one would think is possible.[90] However, as I stated earlier, and have argued throughout, this decrease in violence does not transfer to animals as they are not *in* society. Systems like welfarism allow us to use (and commit violence against) species of all kinds, whilst remaining largely removed from the process. Welfarism unintentionally therefore acts to justify and continue violence. Our kindness, in wanting to exploit non-humans in nicer ways, has led to nicer-sounding animal products and a matching perception that we are indeed treating animals better. But it hasn't actually improved a great deal for animals due to economic barriers (namely welfarism) and has no cultural need to so long as the movement against animal use is stagnated by the variety of much easier options to appease guilt, like flexitarianism. It is perhaps no surprise that the emergence of vegan influencers and cookbooks has done more to increase the vegan portion of supermarkets than campaigns like 'meatless Monday' or other campaigns ever seemed to do. Veganism is rolling now like the snowball analogy suggested it would.

As such, my argument has made the point that not every form of animal ethics is helpful. Whilst we should consider speciesism to be a prejudice as bad as others like sexism or racism, this does not mean that animals are helped in the same way humans are. As we become kinder to each other, society might be helped (though, as mentioned in chapter 5, kindness has its pitfalls). But animals are outside of society; locked away in sheds and cages, or out of view under the sea. Our increasing rationality and kindness only helps them if we intentionally and rationally make it do so, and thus sceptically assess the problems

---

[90] Pinker, 2011.

with animal use *and* welfarism in the first place. At current all our kind-ness is doing is hiding the suffering away, making it more palatable for us humans to view, or making it seem 'better' than before, and so in essence making it seem like progress is afoot and we need not worry.

The realisation that not all animal ethics helps is not limited to the understanding that welfarism is harmful, but also to more modern understandings of campaigns on behalf of animals. Kindness may help to mark a society who is more willing to help animals, but it doesn't currently entail one that is actually helping them. This is more ration-ally formed scepticism at work. It may seem a big step to have to con-sider veganism as a lifestyle change, but feel solace in the fact that the same argument which espouses rational veganism also promotes the opposition of the animal charities which most offend our cultural tastes: groups like PETA or VIVA! with their bunny suits, red paint and anthropomorphic T-shirts are not necessarily allies in rational so-cial change.

Single-issue campaigns

Francione occasionally touches on the problems with single-issue cam-paigns in his published work on welfarism, but never gets near enough to explicitly pointing out their problematic nature. In *Rain Without Thunder*[91] he makes an unnecessary distinction between 'abolitionist' and 'non-abolitionist' single-issue campaigns. Non-abolitionist *single-issue campaigns (SICs)* are those exemplifying the welfarist approach, which aim to regulate animal use (a campaign for free-range eggs ra-ther than battery eggs, for example), whilst abolitionist SICs are those

---

[91] *Rain Without Thunder: The Ideology of the Animal Rights Movement.* Fran-cione, G. L. 1996.

with which one might campaign to abolish a particular animal use (a campaign to end all uses of animals for fur, for example).

Campaigns themselves are useful only as a pragmatic matter. They can help us get closer or further away from what the 'right thing' is. This is where welfarism falls down, but it's also where single-issue campaigns as a whole fall down. A single-issue campaign (of which welfare regulation is just one example) has many negative but necessary effects due to its very structure.

Firstly, it aims to differentiate between different types of animal use. It has to do this, as the aim of any single-issue campaign (for example, to ban the use of wild animals in circuses) is to garner support for that one use without having to campaign for a much harder, more encompassing goal like veganism, or against animal entertainment as a whole. As such, the campaign aims to, and if it is successful it succeeds in, making this one animal use seem worse than others. As a tactical matter this involves the necessary implicit siding with the audience in agreeing all animal use isn't problematic, and then making the case for why this one on its own is problematic. Basically, the campaigns indulge in a meaningful deception, for tactical purposes.

The SIC therefore can't use arguments based on the truth (like 'all animals deserve not to be imprisoned because they are sentient, and speciesism is irrational') and instead makes claims about one species, or the problems with our 'treatment' of animals in this one particular instance, or appeals to our basic emotional views by playing on subjective words like cruelty or compassion. This implicitly agrees that the problem isn't animal use, but rather the method of the use. And hence the SIC has the same effect as welfarism in pushing this idea that animals are our property to use in the first place. It suffers all the same problems that go with welfarism mainly in opposing the social movement 'snow-ball', but also in making people feel better about wider animal exploitation without doing anything significant. In this case because single-issue campaigns rarely are successful, and when they are it is because the animal use in question was so rare in the first place. Take the ban against wild animals in circuses in the UK – a large, concerted effort by animal activist groups that focused on the cuddly looking mega-fauna involved. It seemed to affect around 19 animals in the UK, when it was passed.

One final point to take on board about single-issue campaigns is 'low hanging fruit'. Often these campaigns are referred to like this as the advocates see them as things we can do now, picking off the fruit from the animal exploitation tree one fruit at a time. As Dan Cudahy explains in his popular blog,[92] the problems with this approach are many. First, there are infinite 'fruits' and whilst the advocates are spending huge amounts of resources picking off one, more will grow. After all, they are not advocating the reasons to not use animals, just the reasons not to use them in this one way. Secondly, this acts as 'pruning', allowing the animal industry to remove extremely cruel-looking practices to prune up the rest of the branch of exploitation (e.g. when using wild animals in circuses is opposed, it makes the use of domestic animals in circuses look humane and useful, and often allows the further growth and normalisation of less exotic animal use by al-lowing us to look like we ban the inhumane stuff). Thirdly, every effort to hack at low fruit, or at low branches, is time that could be spent

---

[92] The argument is expanded upon wonderfully in Cudahy's collaboration with Angel Flinn in the essay for The Abolitionist entitled "Single Issue Campaigns: Pruning Exploitation" which can be found here: http://www.theabolitionist.info/article/single-issue-campaigns-pruning-exploitation/

hacking at the roots. Speciesism is pervasive, and fighting it involves spreading the idea that speciesism is a prejudice and is immoral. The truth isn't going to surface with the welfarists' way of implicitly endorsing speciesism, or with the single-issue campaigners' way of taking one fruit at a time (tactically engaging deceit). Animal advocacy that consists of single-issue campaigns is really nothing more than a collection of fabricated reasons why you should do what the advocate handing you the leaflet wants you to do. As a rationalist it is impossible to condone this as a method for advocating any moral cause: emotional or irrational appeals are the entire problem, not the solution, and people aren't going to drop prejudices this way.

Of course, we need only look at further evidence in order to highlight the problems with single-issue campaigns. The animal movement's most successful campaign of all time was the anti-fur campaign. Not only did they manage to make fur socially unacceptable, they also managed to ban its production on UK shores. Yet one brief look at recent news articles shows fur is coming back into fashion. What PETA and the other groups behind these campaigns had managed to do was to make fur socially unacceptable as a fashionable matter by using celebrity endorsements, descriptions of the overly 'cruel' treatment of animals on fur farms, etc. It wasn't 'cool' to wear fur, but PETA were cool. Now PETA have gotten old, and people have grown tired of their wanting to ban not just fur but many types of animal uses under different, random emotional appeals. Suddenly the 'coolness' factor has switched. PETA never attempted to foster a long-term understanding with the problem of animal use, and instead campaigned on these immediately successful 'coolness' arguments. As a result, when the furore dies down, people go back to fur like anything else. The sales have hit new highs in recent years.[93] People never really understood PETA's arguments to be of rational value, because they weren't, so the anger faded as soon as the celebrity advertisements stopped: evidential proof that single-issue campaigns are structurally flawed, by virtue of needing to differentiate themselves from the effective truth, with use of emotive or narrow reasoning. I argued much earlier that we need to be careful with 'emotive' language for rational causes, and the supposed 'success' of the anti-fur campaigns that used it are perhaps the most prevalent warning. This is evidence which is relevant for any moral advocacy, and it asks us to strongly consider indulging rationality rather than short-term tactics, or at least to always include the former.

The irrationality of animal rights groups

A worrying number of animal groups claim that violence and intimidation is a useful tool, or that veganism is about 'being compassionate', 'loving animals', or even that veganism is some ultimate marker of health or natural eating, on top of their attempts to justify welfarism and single-issue campaigns in the face of solid reason. Thus it is little wonder that serious people don't take veganism for the serious obligation that it is. After all, current advocacy on veganism is almost entirely irrational.

This does not mean that veganism isn't to be taken seriously; for the same reason that if atheism had been the preserve of such poor arguments/tactics in history, it shouldn't be ignored on this basis either.

---

[93]   http://www.guardian.co.uk/lifeandstyle/2009/nov/22/fur-rather-go-na-ked "In 2007, fur sales worldwide totalled £10bn, up 11% on the previous year, with nine years of continuous growth. Last year, the fur trade contributed £13bn to the global economy, and although fur farming was banned in Britain in 2003, the UK's fur trade turnover is about £400-500m a year."

It is, though, useful to separate these groups from veganism, as they do not stand up for the same rational veganism that I am advocating here. Over the last few years I've had wonderful support in my criticism of these types of animal rights groups, from a variety of intelligent and rationally valuing people across the world who are in complete agreement with what a rational morality advocates. Unsurprisingly, these kinds of vegans often also value the tenets of anti-theism and rational consistency. Yet these are the precious few and are far outweighed by a vocal majority ignoring any sort of reason-based analysis.

The spiritual ideas put across by animal groups, often focusing on ideas we can generously call 'compassion', manifest themselves even in the best current animal rights theory available. Aforementioned scholar Gary L. Francione, who pioneered most aspects of the abolitionist critique of animal advocacy, is perhaps the best example of this. He states that his theory is not scientifically provable, but rather rests upon 'the truth of non-violence'.[94] Indeed, one wonders why those ideas like welfarism (which he rightly shows to be counter-productive) cannot be justified by the claim that they rest on the 'truth of welfare regulation', if we are going to accept that random spiritual ideas can be valid assumptions. Given the inability to defend welfarism, yet the fervent way groups like PETA indulge in it, this very well may be argued to be their position.

In any case, Francione's assumptions are part and parcel of the reason why people are simply not flocking to veganism in the US, and why vegans themselves are not flocking to 'abolitionism' (which is the position Francione names his own). It even explains why most people

---

[94] http://www.abolitionistapproach.com/new-atheism-and-animal-ethics-some-reflections/

don't bother with morality at all. Literally everyone in society believes that faith is an okay way to form beliefs. Indeed, Francione and the rest of the animal movement appear to embrace this with open arms, happy to argue at a level of immaterial, personal 'truth' which is no better than religious wars that are started over whose God is right on some random issue.

To his credit, Francione rises above much of this arguing from a spiritual basis, by making many of his arguments (like the anti-welfarism arguments, as previously explained) of a rational and evidence-based variety. However, can he really expect many of those who are supportive of welfarism to drop their own 'personal truths' and embrace his rational arguments, when his own position is based on a foundation of 'personal truths' in the first place? So long as the 'truth of non-violence' is all that's holding up his ideas, it's no better than showing Muslims the rationale behind why there is no Allah and expecting them to then start believing in a Christian God. The analogy isn't perfect, and of course some people will still see the problems with welfarism due to Francione's tireless efforts to promote abolitionism, but it's doubtful that such a method will set the world on fire. The fact that 25 years of abolitionist theory has created nothing but a small pocket of abolitionists in each country, while most animal rights people flock to single-issue campaigners like PETA, is perhaps telling. Many of you reading this book before will have heard of veganism, and perhaps even of Peter Singer, but had you heard of Gary Francione?

Conservationism: it isn't about animals

At the start of this chapter I briefly alluded to conservationism as an often-mistaken choice. This is incorrect in some respects.

Conservation of the environment, of green space and of natural animal habitats is entirely necessary, and even morally obligatory. We shouldn't be arrogantly dumping waste around, just as we shouldn't be using resources we don't need to in a world where resources may soon be worryingly thin on the ground.

However, the type of animal conservationism previously mentioned (the type done by the WWF and others) is rather irrational. These groups focus not on the interests of individual sentients, but rather on the interests of biological categories. For instance, the WWF are not concerned with the suffering an individual might feel, but rather with the depletion of a category of animal (a species).

We should treat this claim with extreme caution. A depleting species can be an entirely natural and necessary occurrence. We shouldn't destroy the habitats of sentient individuals, but we also shouldn't be overly concerned about individuals who are naturally dying out simply because they are at an evolutionary dead end (perhaps like pandas, with their disastrously low sex drive and reliance on nutritionally sparse bamboo), so to speak. Yet these groups aim specifically at these species, intending to garner empathy for a biological category rather than the experiencing individuals themselves. This is human empathy getting carried away with itself to a vastly irrational place of no good. Pandas are arguably not better off in zoos, and if they die out whilst we are leaving their habitat alone to give them a chance to live, then what is the problem with this extinction? Many of them don't appear to want to breed.

Take the more radical conservationist and media friendly Sea Shepherd group. They spend millions upon millions rescuing a few whales every year,[95] whilst trillions die in human exploitation of other animals, and whilst many members of the crew of the Sea Shepherd aren't even vegans once they go back to their everyday lives (and so arguably indulge in more needless exploitation than they stop). It is peculiar. The WWF thrives on our earlier mentioned unfortunate inability to differentiate the plight of one individual from the more important plight of many, whilst Sea Shepherd thrives on the donations of rebellious, drama and 'direct-action' loving animal advocates. This is simply not charity, in the same way that wearing a white lab coat doesn't make someone a dentist. The rational moral of the story? You wouldn't pay people to fix your teeth just because they wear white coats, so don't support people in the name of charity just because they claim to be activists.

In all seriousness, we should be concerned that our morality is becoming tied up in category orientated, misanthropic ethics rather than rationally asserted, practical theory. If *rational veganism* is an area of ethics that we should create/jump on board with, conservationism of this type is one it wholeheartedly opposes. As was stated earlier, we need to be very wary of mainstream charities and movements of all types. All animal ethics certainly doesn't help just by virtue of its intention.

While it is irrational to put animals on an intellectual or spiritual pedestal, it is also irrational for us to assert that we can use them as our property in the first place. We have no explicit need to use animals for

---

[95]http://www.theage.com.au/national/how-sea-shepherd-stays-afloat-20120110-1ptu6.html

food, clothing or the variety of other uses we find for them, so justifying this immense level of suffering and death is not logically sound.

I only see one topic – vivisection – where we can justify our use of animals in anything but frivolous terms. But I cannot find moral logic to support this sacrifice of millions of animals for gradual scientific improvement (it is not a case of one animal life in exchange for one human life, as many propose), and I hope that sooner rather than later we can completely replace the remaining numbers of animals in our research. However, even if we conceded a necessity for vivisection, we would still face recognition that 99.9% of the billions of animals we kill each year happen to be completely unnecessary and irrational.

Chapter 7: Determinism and Free Will

In accepting rationality as a basic guide for our behaviour, and accepting morality as a rational, scientific endeavour, there is one big area of current philosophical thought that stands out. That area is determinism and the notion that free will, in the sense that we generally think of it, doesn't actually exist. Like almost every other area of this book, if you aren't familiar with determinism then this isn't going to sit well with your initial intuitions. The counterintuitive initial nature of determinism is one that proves, again, just how fallible even the most seemingly secure of our intuitions are in the face of reason.

However, it has been known for a while now that we live in a world of cause and effect. Science is able to make marvellous advances and technological leaps, and all of this is due to the deterministic nature of the world. If things happened randomly, then science would be at a loss. If when trying to decode the human genome, similar results were different every day, then we wouldn't have gotten far. Similarly, in the world the rest of us inhabit, if we were trying to build a road, and for no reason the consistency of the tarmac varied so as to be unpredictable on a random basis, we couldn't even begin to lay it. Science works in a large part because we can make predictions about anything, based on the fact that it only reacts given certain factors, and not randomly. Causation is as provable as a theory can get.

This is not to say we don't occasionally describe something as random because we don't know how it works, and might never be able to know. But randomness itself is a mythical quality designed to explain this exact human limit of not being able to know. Randomness, like God, is an explanation often utilised when we don't know why something happens. But as a scientific matter, there is no reason to suppose that randomness exists at all. As we will see later, certain areas of science challenge this but do not prove randomness exists.

Free Will

Humans (and other animals, for that matter) are not just objects, but organic life forms that have evolved certain conscious capabilities. We feel pain, and can make decisions in real time based on our experiences. We can also act in real time with our experiences (milliseconds after coming across stimuli) and so can utilise our sentient capabilities to our great benefit; giving us, as animals, a huge advantage over individual plants and other non-conscious organisms in continuing to survive. Imagine us, if you will, as plants that grew the ability to react and run away, or fight others who wanted to eat us.[96] We're much more likely to survive than plants that are rooted to the spot and which can only react gradually to stimuli like sunlight.

This inherent advantage, consciousness, has been philosophised to be many things over the ages (a link to God, a gift of stewardship to

---

[96] I am not making the claim that we were ever plants, in our evolutionary history, though we might have been plants of some sorts at some point.

150

the Earth, etc.[97]). One of those which most societies believe in is that coupled with rationality, consciousness gives us free will. This is the idea that although we evolved from other individuals, and other organisms, with consciousness and rationality came the ability to choose our fate like never before. We have an ability to choose what happens to us, rise above our instincts and live in the world as free agents. Unlike plants, which are guided by basic stimuli, and animals, who are guided by their instincts.

There is much to be said for the way consciousness/sentience sets us apart from other organisms, certainly, and I've so far argued that conscious individuals are the only recipients of morality. However, determinism categorically shows that free will doesn't exist. This is counterintuitive as we feel like we have free will. I look at a dog salivating at food, or a gerbil compelled to chew the cardboard I give to her, and I feel ruled by my instincts to a lesser degree than those two animals are. I believe that because I have a capacity for explicit rationality, my consciousness is of a type through which my choices are not chosen and guided by instinct, but rather chosen by me, as a person who is examining their environment. Yet whilst I am arguably more rationally able, I'm not any less ruled by my genes or my experiences; my thought processes could be infinitely complex, but they are still processes, with which the same input through the same machinery will provide the same output.

Determinism shows that no matter how free we feel, we are still recipients of a rich history of experiences, going all the way back to that

---

[97] Consciousness itself seems to be at the heart of most Abrahamic religion, for instance, with our current and historical inability to theorise what exactly consciousness entails leading to all manner of predictable religious charlatans exploiting this lack of understanding.

time when our parents conceived us. Starting at the beginning, we came into existence as the result of two merging cells (an event not chosen or willed by us in any way, as cells themselves hold no consciousness, never mind rationality) and from that moment on, what happened to us was also not our choice. We didn't choose how our mother carried us in her womb, or where to, and likely the first influence we had on anyone else, as conscious individuals, was instinctually formed when living in the womb: perhaps a kick here or a turn there, which may have influenced our mother's behaviour or the behaviours of other noticing parties. Even if we assume that from that moment of initial, instinctual consciousness that eventually resulted in a movement, we were 'choosing' what happened, we still have never had free will, as that movement *itself* was the result of two cells being formed weeks before we had these conscious instincts, and there have been millions of cellular and environmental happenings since then that we weren't the conscious authors of, and which eventually caused this instinctual kick or movement to happen. As such, there was never a time when we began as a clean slate making a decision; we have always been agents acting from experiences and genetic occurrences which we didn't choose.

From this simple fact we can draw out cause and effect. You kicked not because you randomly or spiritually decided to kick, but because something compelled you to kick; or screamed when you were born not because you randomly or spiritually wanted to scream, but because something compelled you to scream. Cause and effect means that you were never an agent acting free of your genes and experiences, and if you join the dots from any action in your life, you can draw right back to it being the fault of two cells merging, which is in turn the fault of other activities (in this case, an activity by your parents which you probably don't want to think about). No decision you make is truly 'free'. In the same way that every mathematical law – no matter how abstract – can be drawn back to real-world meaning, every decision you make is pre-determined by the experiences, thoughts and actions that led to it.

This has interesting connotations. At every point in your life, in every single nanosecond, every thought going through your head and every decision you intentionally make is the result not of a truly free choice, but rather is predetermined to happen. You think you are making a choice between two different options, but realistically you are choosing no more than the dog is choosing to salivate, the gerbil is choosing to chew the cardboard, or the plant is choosing to bloom. Had every factor been the same (all genetic and worldly experiences had happened in exactly the same way, all thoughts were exactly the same, etc.) you couldn't have chosen to do otherwise at any point. This is no less true for the plant, the gerbil or the dog than it is for you. You, the dog and the gerbil are different to the plant in that you are sentient and the plant is not, but you are the same in not possessing true free will.

Scientific evidence has also begun to support this kind of reason. Libet, et al, in an influential 1983 study, conducted an experiment to discover if cerebral activity could be recorded before we make a decision, to note whether the action is really well on its way to happening before we are aware of it.[98] They categorically discovered that: "The

---

[98] Time of conscious intention to act in relation to onset of cerebral activity (readiness-potential). The unconscious initiation of a freely voluntary act. Libet B, Gleason CA, Wright EW, Pearl DK. 1983. *Brain: A Journal of Neurology.*

onset of cerebral activity clearly preceded by at least several hundred milliseconds the reported time of conscious intention to act." The findings of this study are doubted by some, including those who note that perhaps this shows that the brain is 'aware' and ready to make a decision, not necessarily already deciding before we consciously know. Perhaps they are right. But, however we make sense of the results, there is definitely brain activity there which we are not aware of, which is doing work before we consciously decide on an act. Thus, whichever way one looks at it, we are not the conscious authors of all that happens in our brain. Add this to our knowledge of cause and effect, and there's only one conclusion to draw.

Moral implications

Our lack of free will doesn't mean that we should never punish someone for their actions. A rational morality, as I have explained it, is just that – rational. Allowing a serial killer to walk the streets just because he isn't to blame in a philosophical account of free will is not rational. Sure, we should not punish someone for punishment's sake. This means that if we see no benefit to punishment, in that there is no safety increase for society, no rehabilitative possibility to the punishment, and no far-reaching societal effect in providing a detrimental situation for acting in the immoral way, then the punishment should not be administered. However, it is hard to see how this will impact on most of societal punishment anyway, which is primarily conducted for the above purposes. Punishment is rational even though we might not be to blame for the action which is being punished.

We should, however, bear determinism in mind for the minority situations in which criminals are locked up for no reason. Still, as earlier stated, allowing for individual cases like this to have an effect on general societal rules isn't very practical and might well result in laws being gotten around. So in effect, determinism and our lack of free will may be a subject which is practically null in legal terms. We should take it on board, if individual situations allow without sacrificing a wider ranging rational analysis, but this might not ever even occur.

As a more relevant point, we should be aware of the truth about free will on an individual level. People aren't intrinsically evil, but rather are recipients of the deterministic nature of the universe. As much as people may be to blame for committing an act at a societal level, they are not so much to blame as individuals, but rather we all are responsible as a society. It's our society that has made these persons the way they are, and it is in our interactions with them that we can avoid their becoming obstacles to civilised people. Understanding the nature of determinism, and our lack of free will, allows us to truly see how practical ethics works, and how we are all players in a society grander than our own individual organisms – a society which often creates the problems it is trying to get rid of. Understanding our role in creating these problems, and the rational nature of being generally 'nicer' or more respectful perhaps, is something vital to any successful moral code. Society should be taught that we need to punish people, and that it isn't anger, but sympathy that should be going the way of the punished party. Punishment is a useful concept unless we reach a state where people are all rational machines, but it is not a philosophically sound result of analysing 'fault'.

It seems that whenever a rational idea is disliked on personal grounds, ideas like quantum theory are wheeled out, caked in misapprehension and relieved of central limbs, to back up the opposition. Just as I'm sure that critics will point to fictional, media labelled 'perfect rationalists' like Dr. House, MD, or any cold yet brilliant detective in order to argue that rationality does not cause kindness, I'm sure that they will mutilate quantum theory and then show its half-dismembered carcass as a reason why determinism doesn't exist, and why we all have free will.

The argument – as dissected in earlier chapters – will state that science has uncovered activity at particle level which does not appear to act in a 'cause and effect' manner, and thus the universe, which is made up of an innumerable number of particles, is not based on cause and effect either.

In all honesty, even if particle physics did turn out to be an area in which randomness does exist, it wouldn't say anything about determinism. We can carry out an infinite number of experiments on humans to show that they are influenced by the world around them and are created by genes, and given that we know thoughts don't appear at random we can be fairly certain that determinism exists. So even if subatomic particles appear to act randomly, they are obviously not affecting our actions as larger entities in any meaningful way as *we* don't appear to act randomly. Indeed, no area of science appears to act randomly, and everything is made of supposedly random subatomic particles. At worst, this shows that the subatomic world is not disintegrating our physical laws at societal level, and so is not affecting our deterministic natural universe. But more likely is that this level of science (which exists at base level in everything) is simply not yet understood properly.

It would be odd that our building blocks were not somehow explainable, and various physicists around the world are working on ironing out this interesting problem right now.

Similarly, particle activity isn't necessarily random just because it appears random in some aspects. Throughout history, science has continually solved seemingly paradoxical instances and has many times turned the 'assumed random' into the 'rationally caused'. Particle physics seems like a whole different kettle of fish, however, given that which subatomic particles make up (larger objects) do act in a cause and effect way, and given that which we know about science couldn't have been established without the law of cause and effect. In turn, it would mean billions of observations and results couldn't have been explained by following these laws. You can't dump thousands of years of consistent truth finding because of one area seeming anomalous. Perhaps particle physics is anomalous, or perhaps we just don't yet understand how it isn't. Either way, we are very likely to uncover better ways to answer these questions.

Does determinism mean we shouldn't bother?

Many people believe that if determinism is true, then why bother at all? Indeed, if we can never truly choose otherwise, why choose at all? What we do is already determined to happen.

This kind of problem comes up in two ways. Firstly, fatalism: the idea that if we are already determined, there is nothing we can do to change our fate, and so we shouldn't bother. This is a logical fallacy. Determinism explains how if things were to happen in exactly the same way again, they couldn't happen differently and you couldn't choose differently. It does not mean we do not have a choice at the social level, it just means we couldn't have chosen differently, had things been the same again.

This doesn't mean that we should just stop, as everything is already decided. Nothing is decided, and there is no great plan. Even if we were in a state of perfect technology and understanding, and could figure out what the future would look like starting from now, it would already be different to what we have theorised as our very understanding of it changes its result. We are determined to act in certain ways as a result of previous events, but we are not fated to act in a certain way so that certain events couldn't change some determined fate. There is a slight, but distinct difference.

The second result of this argument is not so much fatalism as 'excusitarianism', if I may invent such a concept. This is not that we are fated to act a certain way, but rather that we couldn't act any other way, so why bother doing anything nice/stressful/hard. Essentially it is misunderstanding what determinism means. If you are acting like a twit, you probably couldn't have acted like anything but a twit if the same set of circumstances were to happen again. However, going forwards, you may or may not act like a twit depending on what you choose to do. You are still free to choose to act like a twit, or to refrain, it's just that your genes and experiences are the reason for the choice rather than your immortal soul or evil nature. The kinds of free will excusitarianism pretends doesn't exist, actually still do. Not in a non-deterministic sort of way, but we still affect the world by acting, and thus excusitarianism is just a misunderstanding – it thinks that we don't affect the world.

Excusitarianism makes little sense. It is essentially a pragmatic theory, trying to excuse one's actions by reference to the fact you couldn't have chosen to do otherwise. But excuses are fairly unimportant when the punishment for societally immoral actions is not given based on fault. So long as the punishment itself is based on the consequential basis for the punishment (like security, rehabilitation or deterrence), rather than on some notion of punishing just because it's a person's fault, then the excusitarian position is illogical. There's no benefit to being an excusitarian, just as there is no logical reason to be one. Yes, we are creatures of cause and effect, but that doesn't mean that our actions don't still have an effect on ourselves and others. You couldn't have chosen to do otherwise, but it's still important that you choose one way and not the other most of the time. Moreover, you can still be punished for acting immorally, so excusitarianism is fruitless.

Free will as a delusion of rationality

Just as religious and spiritual belief can be shown to be an error of rationality (a desire to find truth in the face of seemingly unanswered questions) so can the belief of free will. People don't like what a world without free will would look like, and that lack of affection comes from a misunderstanding of that world.

Spiritualism argues against determinism, as it doesn't like the idea that there is no god pulling the strings, or no spiritual sphere we can float away in. Alternatively, fatalism and excusitarianism are positions which oppose free will because they don't like what they think it entails: concerns which are comforted by analysis of the facts and dissolving of the myths.

As I have argued throughout, we make our decisions and form our positions rationally, and on determinism that is no different. As important as it is to understand why determinism is true, and why we

don't hold a classical notion of free will, it is also important to understand why people choose any of the excuses or positions against it. They
do so as they believe it rational in order to continue either:

- their perceived rationally formed moral codes. Like in the case
  of religion/spirituality, where they feel morality is rational but can
  only fathom the spiritual reasons for it, and so want to twist things
  like determinism that disprove spiritual ideas,

or

- their perceived rational reasons for acting. In the case of Fatalism and Excusitarianism, whose proponents genuinely believe
  determinism to be illogical in disallowing them to act in the way
  that they feel they can.

It's important to undertake this exercise at any stage in a rational
theory of morality, as it allows us to see how people are making decisions rationally, and so are valuing rationality at every point, and moreover so we can see that the problem is a lack of rational consistency or
understanding of the consequences.

The pro-social benefits of feeling free?

There is a study (by no means the only one on this subject) authored
by Baumeister et al.,[99] which claims that a belief in free will may "foster
a sense of thoughtful reflection and willingness to exert energy, thereby
promoting helpfulness and reducing aggression, and so disbelief in free
will may make behavior more reliant on selfish, automatic impulses and
therefore less socially desirable." Indeed, there are a number of studies
which claim to show similar results. Does this mean that it is rational
to pragmatically trick people into believing they have free will?

---

[99] http://psp.sagepub.com/content/35/2/260.short

Firstly, as specified a number of times, if morality is to be considered science it can't very well fudge results. We can feel at liberty to have societies where punishments occur, but we're also rationally obliged to tell people that we do this not out of blame, but because we need to protect one another. Tricking people into believing irrational ideas, as a tool for keeping people nice and helpful, is questionable, whilst not particularly honest or consistent. Sure, rational morality appears to have pragmatic benefits in every area, but at the same time the scientific aspect should always outweigh the pragmatic. This comes from a scientific understanding: we don't fly to the moon sitting on banana skins, because it is scientifically impossible. Whilst moral science doesn't make it physically impossible to act in immoral ways, it does make it morally impossible. So while it may be scientifically possible to deceive people en masse, for political reasons, it is not morally rational in the way I've argued that rational morality must be. Put simply, physical science defines what we physically can and cannot do. Moral science defines what we should and should not do. Rather than pragmatically fudging results in either, we are obligated to be rational.

Secondly, as a practical matter, the reason the earlier mentioned experiments get the results they do is precisely because of the myths about determinism; myths I have so far debunked, which manifest in the four spheres of Religious, Spiritual, Fatalist and Excusitarianist. The latter two are the kinds of behaviour which experiments seem to show exist from belief in determinism, but the experiments themselves are flawed precisely because they do not explain, and more importantly foster an understanding, that determinism does not imply fatalism and excusitarianism. People intuitively believe determinism does imply fatalism, upon hearing that free will doesn't exist, and these ideas need rational analysis to be debunked. Rational analysis results in rational understanding; something which is not allowed for in the method or the timespan of these experiments. Were the experiments to explain the reasons why determinism doesn't mean fatalism, and why it doesn't lead to excusitarianism either, and the participants were able to come to terms with what it rationally does involve in due time, one can be sure the findings would be different. Indeed, experiments in which anyone's basic moral beliefs were shown to be false would be likely to result in the findings that these experiments on determinism show – a dejected outlook on what life without dearly held beliefs would be like – so allowing participants the time to adjust to the rational truth that morality still exists, would be the key to avoiding the problems.

As a final point, would it even be creating a morally able society if we deceived people into acting well by invoking ideas like free will or any other mythical concepts? It might, at least in the short term. However, as with the problems of a society that believes in religion (and the faith-based problems that go with) making people act in a nice way through deception is not really what we want, is it? Don't we want people to understand the world, strive to know more about it, and act nicely because they truly believe it is the rational and honest thing to do? The way to this world is by enlightening people with reality, not treating them like they can't handle the truth.

***

We still live, we still feel, we are still conscious, and morality is still rational. We just have to admit that our lives happen on top of scientific laws, not outside of them. Free will doesn't add meaning, and if we don't act well we will be determined to irrational, immoral lives, just as if we do act well we will be determined to more rational, moral lives. Determinism doesn't change this; it just helps to see that we are all responsible, to some degree, for each other as well as ourselves. This fundamentally changes the way we should view morality.

We don't know what we are determined to do, and everything we learn and act out changes our future significantly, just like it did prior to accepting determinism. The difference is that we are discovering our futures as agents consisting of only genes and experiences, rather than as spiritually immaterial, blame and praise-worthy souls.

Chapter 8: Politics

If we were to adopt a way of determining moral values rationally, then it would be much easier to create useful and successful structures. In other words, a rational politics becomes a possibility. Politics, after all, is a way of organising and ruling society. If we have guiding principles for society, and a way of determining explicit human values, then it stands to reason that we can develop a more rational system of politics with which to implement our values. This section will explore what a rational political system might look like if we had rational morality.

Do we need an organised system?

If we start right at the bottom, we must start with the question of whether we need an *organised* system of politics at all. Anarchism famously states that we should reject hierarchies and power structures in every form, as they inhibit our freedom, which is one of our guiding foundational principles of ethics. Anarchists tend to state, instead, that society should be an organisation of voluntary cooperation.

There are many different forms of anarchism, but primarily they share a belief that government is not necessary, that freedom is the most important aspect. This is not particularly contentious: if we could arrange a society without imposing governments, or legal and judicial systems, in which sentient individuals could flourish as well or better than they would inside more organised systems, then we should do so.

Freedom appears to be an important part of well-being, so undoubtedly a belief in its importance is correct. The former belief, that government is not necessary, is less persuasive. In terms of judging anarchism's usefulness for this theory, we should judge specifically whether we can create more well-being without a government. Could we ensure the principles of protection and fairness as well? This is something I find little evidence for.

The evidence on side of anarchism is, as already stated, that its vision of a functioning, cooperative society is less forceful and thus more conducive to well-being than one in which we have to force people to do things, or punish misbehaviour, or even provide resource-based reward for employment. However, this is simply an ideal utopia. The method for achieving it is not so easy to grasp. It is supposed that through education we can teach people the respect and knowledge needed to create this society. Is this even possible?

In one sense, it seems not. After all, even if we one day see moral science as accepted, and thus create an evidence-based moral code, we will never become perfect moral decision makers ourselves – we earlier discussed, at length, that we can never become perfect moral decision-making machines. We are not gods, we are subjects of a rich evolutionary history which has also left us with implicit imperfections and biases. We do need set rules to guide us at some stage so as we don't follow blind bias on different moral issues: especially new moral issues. It is difficult, if not impossible, to imagine a non-hierarchical or non-authority-based system that could be used to eliminate bias in this way. Science has never gotten close to it, despite huge levels of education in some areas, and the rules of the scientific method have always been required.

The perfect form of hierarchy might be loose, or incredibly civilised, but there are so many different aspects to life in human society that we surely need some form. Experts on environmental science, for example, are better judges of it than simply interested or even non-interested parties. They should be the ones imparting the laws about how we treat the environment, or at least helping to create a top-level guide for passing down, and there is no reason to suppose this kind of informed hierarchy is problematic.

This doesn't necessarily negate the idea of anarchism, however it does negate the more extreme forms which would have no organised rules at all. Furthermore, as anarchism should see no end for a need to science itself (unless we take the even less rational forms of anarchism which promote returning to a non-technological wilderness – a highly spiritual idea), we thus must imagine that even a perfect society would *at least* have to involve the kind of structure that good science demands. Yet this is always going to be a hierarchy, whereby non-scientists' opinions are taken as less valuable than those of extremely well-educated scientists in any one particular area. Reason provides this type of authority within science. This is a necessary hierarchy with a fairly rigid structure; it is not clear how this is necessarily immoral, other than as a baseless correlative assumption due to the observed negative effects of instances where power is abused in current society.

Without a doubt we need this scientific structure, at least, so in a rational analysis of what a good political system should be, we are getting further and further from an anarchist view of the world. Until we have evidence that hierarchy is *necessarily* harmful, even in a more developed and morally rational world, then we don't have reason for rejecting it. Still, anarchism – of a much diluted type – is an option. We must consider whether we can find better ideas than anarchism in more organised and less voluntary structures, though – structures closer to our current governments – before we start hacking at and moulding anarchism as a potential successor.

Authoritarian structures

It almost seems a little pointless to consider an authoritarian structure, given the moral principles we have put in place. Authoritarian governments have, historically, been the place of various forms of fascism which have not boded the well-being of complex groups of individuals. It's not clear how enforcing the will of dictators or controlling groups on large population would help to further our principle of freedom and autonomy, so it seems to suffer as significant, though very opposite, problems as anarchism does.

Still, it makes sense to explore it because we are not speaking about history, we are asking what is a good system with which to roll out rules based on moral science. Similarly, in exploring the options which don't work we find a better idea of what might.

As basic theory goes, authoritarianism could only have an argument for being an option in one very strict sense – a dictatorship which did nothing but employ moral scientists to work out moral rules, and then enforce them via its network of strict control. That all sounds very well, but how could it work? The entire point of moral science is an open and evidence-based nature. Everyone should be able to challenge moral rules if they have reason or evidence to do so and we would surely want channels to do this. After all, remember that we are trying to make morality a science so as it doesn't make as many errors. Science explicitly opens its doors to new ideas regardless of who says them or whether or not the establishment disagrees. The role of the authoritarian in science isn't taken by people or structures, it is taken by truth; the only possible authoritarian factor in science, in any sense, is truth.

With that said, once again we are trying to twist and bend the definition of the political idea to fit into the kind of rule which moral science would allow for. Once we change authoritarianism to include such characteristics as 'open to changing its mind based on the ideas of the people' we really had better stop and just look somewhere else, as it no longer resembles the definition of authoritarianism. We've already taken off both its central limbs; the torso of authoritarianism is clearly not suitable for injecting moral science into.

Rule by the few

It is actually quite interesting to consider the forms of government theory that are categorised under a 'rule by the few' option; also known as 'aristocracy'. We can immediately discount things like Stratocracy (rule by the military) or Plutocracy (rule by the wealthy) as the military and the wealthy have no authority to be a ruling class under moral science, and they seem irrelevant. We'd be looking for something that could roll out moral rules, and help in forming committees to discuss them, perhaps. How about more general aristocracy, also known as 'rule by an elite'?

We can immediately find reasons to ignore the idea of unelected or unqualified aristocracy, as these don't make a great deal of sense for our uses; they are just arbitrary elitism, and we need to allow people to live in both fair and free ways. But what about governance by the most qualified, in which the people in each area of government are genuinely some of the most qualified for that job? This is undoubtedly something which, on a basic level, would fit with moral science. Our current societies are extremely flawed by the fact that we don't elect people who are qualified for political jobs; we elect people almost in popularity contests. Political parties currently put forward PR-friendly individuals, from whom we choose, half-politically and half-personality, who we like.

Once again, to be thorough, we should note that we might be bending the historical definition of 'aristocracy' a little here. In modern times aristocracy has been about people of privilege getting positions of power. We see it with monarchs and unelected forms of government (even in the UK's House of Lords, where people are simply handed positions of power due to their influence in society) but it also has an effect in parliament. The people in the cabinet at any given time are not often the leaders of any particular academic field, and certainly not moral philosophers or ethicists; they are people who have been to the right finishing schools and universities that breed the right type of person – not the right type of qualification – for a role in getting elected to government. Again, this sounds like a cynical opinion, but the fact that we have such a narrow focus of business and politics trained people in government should be a case and point. I will discuss this business aspect more on the discussion in economics, but the politics side is damning – politics should be about an ability and vast amount of knowledge in one area, with which to weigh decisions in that area. Arguably, political study itself is barely even necessary for someone going into politics. At least not in a system which is fair and rational.

The minister in charge of health should be educated in and knowledgeable about health, whilst being a proven authority and/or decision maker in that sector. Someone rationally able to judge decisions and weigh options in public medicine. And someone who shares the value of the population in a rational manner. At current, in the UK at least, this is not how ministers are picked. Far from it. Ministers are firstly picked by having the right political allegiance, secondly by having the necessary loyalty or passion to that allegiance and thirdly by having a large amount of either experience or potential to become a loved public figure for that allegiance. At no point is the country scoured for the best person to judge and make decisions about the health care sector; indeed, we are lucky if the person chosen has any experience at all with it, as the post is handed out almost like a workplace promotion for political party loyalty. Within which ministers are then shuffled around for years, like a dysfunctional office, where the manager, admin and reception staff all move positions regularly.

Still, the type of aristocracy we have briefly developed here makes an awful lot of sense in terms of moral science. Picking people to do the jobs which they are the most qualified to do is a sensible solution, so aristocracy is a viable option which should be on the table. We need to ask if there's anything better, or any further factors which should be included in a rational political structure.

Democracy

Democracy will be the most easily understood form of politics to almost everyone reading this, as most of you will live in a country with a government that is run this way. Loosely speaking, of course. Politics is difficult to define and depending on the given checklist, your government can range from democratic, to authoritarian, to plutocratic. But, roughly defined, most countries appear to now be democratic in some way.

There are various reasons for this widespread democracy. Partly this is due to Western influence. The US and a handful of European countries have been fairly strict with many authoritarian regimes, perhaps in fear of a third and potentially Earth-destroying world war, and thus have pushed democracy in both a political and military manner. A democracy, it is believed, is a way of best avoiding the kind of rigid, unchangeable opinions that lead to escalating conflict. There are various reasons for that which are not necessary to go into here, but safe to say that if a government is scared of upsetting the voters – for fear of not being elected again – they will (at least in theory) be scared of making extreme decisions.

What democracy consists of varies greatly, like most other theories. The UK has a representative democracy in which we elect people to make decisions on our behalf, whilst others have a more direct democracy in which the people themselves have a bigger say in decisions. The latter, of course, tends to be less favoured the bigger a society gets. We don't all have time to discuss and vote on every single issue, so we elect people to do it for us.

The advantage of democracy for this theory is in its ability to share power with everyone. A democracy is an attempt to take everyone's opinions into account – something moral science is also about – without making everyone attend parliament or vote on political decisions every day. There is no doubt that this is a very sensible move, especially in the current world climate. Holding people to account is very important.

The problem with democracy in moral science is twofold. Firstly, a democracy theoretically allows for people to vote for their own interests, however small. So you can get a tyranny of the majority – in the sense that if most people vote for something which mildly improves their lives, whilst catastrophically affecting others (say building a new theme park, over the site of several human homes and several animal habitats), the motion can pass.

Of course democracy often gets around this with moral code: by being a part of society people implicitly accept its laws, and thus accept that they are not allowed to make certain decisions a matter of democracy. Some things are just wrong. If we bring in the current method of judging morality with moral science, then democracy works even better. Nevertheless, this shows us that the most extreme forms of democracy are not viable. This would rule out systems whereby moral rules are set by trends and opinions to the degree that even the most sensible moral laws – such as those against unsolicited murder – are amended based on public whim, which can be whipped up by media storms. Democracy is important, but so is educated decision-making and following the rules of rationality: democracy and aristocracy must be merged in a way which both inform one another.

A democratic aristocracy?

We can't really use authoritarian methods of government in this theory, they don't seem to work. Anarchism seems too idealist, at least as a practical matter, and focuses too much on one principle (freedom) over the other two (protection of interests and fairness). However, we can learn from it that freedom is important to human well-being; the strength of feeling anarchists have for freedom supports that freedom is an essential part of human morality. Thus the two theories that best fit into what we need are aristocracy and democracy. Actually, if we were to merge the two together, taking the most relevant parts of each, we could form a fairly substantial spine of a political system.

We need to keep the democratic nature of government. Politicians have to be accountable to people, else we risk allowing for exploitation and thus remove the rational check on authority that democracy provides. However, this isn't enough; most of us are neither educated enough in every area of politics to make rational decisions on who is best to rule us, nor do we have time to be. Politicians should be elected based on looking out for all of our interests, otherwise we risk corruption and defiled levels of well-being; however, we do need a safeguard to make sure we are both educated enough to be making the electoral decisions and that we are selecting from a qualified pool of people rather than being ruled with no say on what's going on.

This is where things get tricky. How do we test the qualifications and abilities of politicians without leaving it to someone more qualified, who is unaccountable? If we 'check the checker', who checks the check on the checker? We get ourselves into a never-ending problem. Similarly, how do we ensure the population is educated in the right areas to be making a decision on who is best in the first place? This involves a new, clever and circular system which ensures no one is unaccountable and every area is scrutinised.

The latter question is perhaps easiest to answer. We need to educate all people in both moral science and rational politics. Implicit in this is the fact that science education itself also needs to be more robust and deserves a place of higher value in schools. We need a society in which people judge evidence-based decision-making as really important, and thus they understand the need for reason. If we all valued these things – which themselves are founded on good evidence – we'd be in a much better place to make political decisions. At the moment our democracies do represent a kind of tyranny of the majority type situation, in which we each represent only our own interests, and usually only in a relatively shallow assessment: rarely do we look at what principles of human civilisation we really value, and too often we get swept up in hysteria about immigration or budget deficits which we otherwise might not, given a better understanding of reason.

This is not surprising, given the lack of trust we each have in our political system: the method of politics itself seems only just better than the untrustworthiness of our politicians. But can we be surprised by or blame voter apathy, shallow decision-making or value-less politicians when the entire system seems to be on a road to nowhere? A system of rational politics means we have a good method, a fairly well-researched plan and an ability to change based on new evidence. This is something which is easy to learn about and even easier to put our trust in.

The first question – how to ensure we are electing qualified politicians – is a much more difficult dilemma. We can at least put down the basics, though, and part of that, once again, is noting that we currently do it wrong.

Political parties are not a good way to run society, yet at current these are how politicians generally get 'qualified' for election. At least in the US and most of Europe, members of the ruling elite are put forth for election almost solely by a political party, and in most cases these come from two or three separate large parties. The candidates are chosen not by how good they are at making decisions on society's behalf, but rather based on how far they hold the same policies as the party. This means that in each society our interests are primarily forced into two or three sets of beliefs, by which a representative sample of our views are meant to appear due to the political fight between the two or three sides on different decisions. Or, in other words, pick the party which best represents your personal opinions out of these three choices, which exist for no other reason than they existed at the last election, everyone else will do the same, and hopefully the resulting mixture will somehow benefit society.

Even on a basic level we can see that this isn't the best possible way of making decisions at a public level. The policies each party holds are, in turn, influenced by the history of the party and the media/majority decisions, not to mention the wealthy donors who allow them to publicise themselves in the best way, and as a result we never seem to be in a place to make good decisions based on the evidence. At best, most of us who vote in elections opt for what we perceive as the lesser evil. This is not what politics should be about. The lesser evil? It's no wonder we've lost our motivation.

We must do away with this 'party' system. On top of everything else it's a way of making people believe dogma and stops us finding better opinions: in the same way that religions force sets of beliefs rather than individual thought, so do political parties. We shouldn't be taking a conservative opinion, a republican opinion or a liberal opinion; we should be taking a rational opinion based on the caveat that we should maximise the well-being of sentient individuals. And we should debate all political opinions by reference to our shared, basic moral principles.

It isn't enough, though, to just criticise what we have; we need a solution. A better political method would be to start using science. Science doesn't have particular problems with corruption because the method checks for and removes it automatically. The issue in using scientific structure in government is that you still need to elect officials to actually make the decisions: whilst scientific decisions are made largely by consensus, it can take years and there is often no pronounced point at which agreement is made. We need the opposite to happen in politics: if we find out there is a flood, we need a structure in which someone is responsible for immediately sending response teams, and this needs to be accountable further up to people explicitly deciding on whether we need response teams and equipment before the event, or what the budget will be, etc. We cannot run any sort of actual parliament entirely consensually, like in science, but science can certainly be used in the selection process, or in keeping politicians in line. Science can give us solutions, and lend us parts of its methodology.

Scientific-influenced selection

So to solve the selection issue, let's create an academic field to study how we should best select politicians, and an academic field for what we even need politicians for. Undoubtedly, when we have moral science we need a slight restructure in legal terms – new decisions should be based on rationality, not necessarily tradition or precedent (though perhaps the current legal system fits nicely into new forms of morality; a thorough examination by our greatest legal minds is required). But we also need to consider what a politician is useful for in light of subjective values being obsolete in favour of moral science. Politicians traditionally make decisions based on values when facing difficult situations, and although we might still need this in situations where a quick resolve is required, undoubtedly it should be moral scientists involved in making this decision – we thus need experts of new types involved. Similarly, scientists and academics of all sorts are vital to take positions in each political area. Perhaps we can make use of current structures within science to fill these roles, but more likely we need to fund public research into each area, which is liable only to the public well-being and thus is choosing independently. Agriculture, health, welfare; there is no government area which should not be run by experts in the academic fields.

How do we set up independent committees and groups in order to study each area of government (as well as the qualification process), presumably run by unelected officials, which are not simply at the authoritarian mercy of those people in charge of running them? The only test for this is absolute scientific transparency. Though respected and well-paid positions are undoubtedly necessary, these should be considered no more specialist and powerful than normal scientists. Thus every inch of their work should be transparent and every decision that is made in the public interest should be methodologically explainable – at a very basic level this means only having to note what the pros and cons were, how they were weighed up, and how the answer or result was tested for validity. This method, in turn, would be open to scrutiny by academia, and at least small grants given to universities in order to employ academics to study every area.

Practical examples

So far we have explored what a rational aristocratic democracy would look like, as a decidedly philosophical matter. This was, in equivalence, an attempt at the philosophy of moral science in government. However, as a theorist, I would like to examine some examples of what this looks like; we need more than a brief idea or ambiguous philosophical notion of change. We have to truly understand and be able to at least

imagine how a process would actually work in real life if we are to plan
it out with the help of specialists in academia. I will set out an example
of how the process might work, along with an idea of how practical it
is to make this change to the current system.

The process of change

Firstly, we would need to replace the political party system with something more capable of providing good, knowledgeable decision makers.
Obviously we are not starting society from scratch, and we already use
the political party system, so the change should be gradual and practical.

We must begin with studying each area of current political decision-making with a view to creating a list of areas we need to replace
(a list which is open to change in the future). The current government
system is a good place to start; they might be the result of a poor and
largely unexamined system, but they do have to make the decisions in
society; as a result they are roughly informed by our needs. By examining what current government departments exist we have a good frame
of what areas our new system has to take on. This will begin with the
most important areas in any society such as healthcare, crime and punishment, education and energy, but also include all other areas which
government currently preside over, such as sport and culture.

From here we have a list of the important areas which need governing. So our first step should be in creating structures within universities, wider academia and the media which specifically study each of
these areas. For many, the job will be relatively easy: medical and legal
departments may need to take on or slightly restructure staff who focus
on government policy already. The academic systems for this analysis

and education are already widespread, a slight change of focus is all that is required. In areas such as sport where there may not be academic analysis already, we may not need the same number of academic analysts and educators as in areas like healthcare, but we still need to see a system whereby potential ministers can be educated and current ministers can be scrutinised.

It is this planning and slight restructuring that must take place first. We need to offer education in these areas, ensure the wealth of existing structures are objective and scientific in approach, and create something which will allow a switch to a better system a few years down the road. We are not realistically talking about more than five to ten years, as we must recognise that we already have experts in all of the important fields: a simple change of perspective is all that is required to make these people potential candidates for election and for running transparent academic checks on the system.

A local problem?

One thing to note is that the system I have so far argued on behalf of would seem to encounter problems in taking into account local interests. For example, if we are voting to elect people to run certain departments, who takes care of and has knowledge of the local issues which current MPs are elected to do?

This problem is also easily solvable. Whilst we are electing people to run and be involved in the decision-making systems of each area of government policy, we can still have elected representatives whose job is to simply listen to and represent the concerns of local people. Problems will be heard as well as they are now, the difference is that we will have educated and better qualified people both making the decisions

179

and better organising/integrating policy with an overall goal in mind. Theoretically this allows not just for better decision-making about local processes at a national level, but also a better local system of councillors which can mimic the national system, not to mention theoretically less waste and more effective spending of taxes with which it can improve services. Evidence-based decision-making has many benefits. We will no longer be serving political whims or personal opinions, which we spend billions flip-flopping between and changing policies unnecessarily every four years, but instead working for a better society under constant, transparent scrutiny.

Checks on government

At elections people would choose between candidates selected not by political parties, but by universities and other institutions putting forth candidates who are educated in these areas. The public do not choose based on the policies or agendas of these people, but rather based on their achievements and their publicly available CVs. And every four years their progress and plans are evaluated in the academic and media sections, whilst the public are given the chance to stick with them or remove them.

After election these people are not unaccountable, but under constant scrutiny from academic institutions. Elections occur every few years, like in the current system, when the MP is up for re-election against new (or previously beaten) candidates; at which point the MP's activities are up for debate, and measured against the achievements of their opponents.

This system is not immune to corruption or bias, and it will be immediately obvious that the role of political parties is being, in a way, replaced by universities and academic institutions. Whilst all those in political academic positions must be transparent and scientific in their undertakings (thus justifying criticism, not just mudslinging) there is arguably still room for bias on their parts – against the elected candidates from other universities, and in favour of their own. This requires a careful balance and universities should be rewarded for scrutinising each other's criticisms, as well as scrutinising the decisions of the MPs. Universities should also be responsible and compensated for challenging the decisions of MPs that they put forward themselves, so as to stop the party loyalty. By allowing for excessive transparency, funding universities independent of results, rewarding valid criticism and punishing mudslinging or unscientific method (which is commonplace, perhaps even the main activity, in current politics), we should be able to strike a balance which minimises bias and maximises a useful political science in every area.

As a final caveat, whilst friendly rivalry is no bad thing, we should also reward universities for cooperation and co-researched projects, as well as the checks also set out above. It is no doubt, yet again, a balance which must be struck, but neutrality and maximising society's potential requires the sharing of knowledge and experience. Keeping neutrality and insuring against bias might sound like a difficult balance to strike, yet when we consider the failures of the current system to do either on a basic level, it is obvious that this new system gives hope. The whole process starts with institutions that are funded purely for teaching students the value of neutrality and science. Humanity has found no better way of achieving progress and minimising human bias than through science, so whilst it may never be perfect, rational politics would arguably be a massive step in the right direction.

Non-transparent policy

The issue of transparency is useful and necessary for moral science, yet somewhat of a hot potato in wider society at the moment. In recent years there has been no shortage of debate on government secrecy. The likes of Julian Assange, Edward Snowden and Bradley/Chelsea Manning have very much brought the issue of 'necessary' national secrets to light. All three of these names are the target of punishment by governments for disclosing official and military secrets, and at the time of writing at least one has received a 30+ year prison sentence for doing so.

Given that the essence of this new political system has been in transparency, with academic institutions allowed access to the methodology of all political decisions, then we must decide if it is necessary for the new system to allow for secrecy in this way and/or whether the system is still capable when we examine 'necessary secrets'.

This is a difficult subject to judge, purely because official secrets remain just that: secret. Without wanting to get into the moral debate, which I cannot be well informed enough on this specific topic to do, it is possible (if necessary) for rational politics to include secrecy on some level. We could restrict transparency to only those who need to know by the threat of punishment, as we do at the moment. It is not ideal, and it must be kept to an absolute minimum if it is needed at all, for which there needs to be an awful lot more work done. But given that it is currently one of the most morally debatable aspects of government, the fact that it would be one of the most morally debatable aspects of a better system of government does not mean that it is a problem with that new system of government so much as a problem inherent in all modern government. Perhaps (and it is just a 'perhaps') our current world situation requires this problematic aspect in any government, no matter how capable.

What is for sure is that we must prioritise holding a rational debate, including the details of at least some previously kept secrets, and examine both the reasons why it might be necessary to keep them secret and the potential problems of doing so. Transparency is an absolute must in rational government, so to exclude any part of national or international rule from transparency is a huge issue if it is not absolutely necessary. It stands to reason that we can historically assess national secrets, whilst problem solving methods for allowing transparency.

Potentially, of course, the common sense theory would be that secrecy is primarily required in order to protect citizens from an outside threat. In the modern world we have seen legal action against the project Wikileaks for exactly this reason, as governments have argued that the divulging of secrets has risked their national security or else encouraged others to do so in the future. If this is the case, and the lack of transparency is justified under these grounds, then we must find ways of internationally soothing this problem. As an idealistic point one might suggest befriending international enemies or rolling out wealth so that it is no longer the case that outsiders provide such threat, thus allowing for safety in transparency. Perhaps I am being naïve. However, I am very aware that a lack of knowledge on these secrets which we protect can, and probably will, stop the theorising towards better levels of public security. It is not just a concern for a more rational theory of politics, as I have stated, but the point of theorising a new system of politics is to solve the problems with the current one. The issue of transparency is currently a problem, and rather than punishing those

183

who fight for transparency, it would be a priority to find a way of solving the issue.

The role of media

The function of the media is to inform and provide news to the population. The effect of owner and shareholder corporate bias in the current media system is well known and it is vital to combat this and do something to ensure media neutrality if we wish for a successful, rational and effective form of politics. We all have jobs to do, we all have roles to fulfil, and in any democracy we cannot all be involved in or informed of every political decision. For society to function when there are millions of us cooperating, we need the media to summarise, report and use journalistic integrity to investigate policies, plans and intentions.

If our journalists were currently just bad at this, it would be one thing. That wouldn't be a systemic problem, but more a problem, perhaps, with our talent pool. But several sources manage to do an admirable job. Sources like the *Guardian* or the *BBC*, even the *Independent*, do provide analysis and use economic or political experts to get news to us – they largely have journalistic integrity, even if they struggle to understand what 'neutrality' means when it comes to climate change, for instance.

The problem is more visible with tabloids, or market-owned newspapers, though. We rely on news media to inform us neutrally, otherwise we have little to no check on our politicians, yet many newspapers are owned and influenced by large moguls who have opinions which they can use newspapers to spread. So the vital job of news media is not fulfilled, and instead we have ended up with unelected moguls and conglomerates who can push their own opinions to their editorial staff. Biasing our opinions of what the facts are, and what is important, and even allowing certain news sources to ignore big stories altogether, whilst publicising others which are barely newsworthy at all. These are people who are unelected, largely unaccountable, and yet wield more power than our democratically elected representatives.

Partly, of course, we can blame the owners and shareholders, but partly it's also an economics problem. We should not be surprised by the rise in 'clickbait' news, in which people are enticed into reading a story purely due to the sensationalism of it, when the only current incentives for media sources are in making money. The way to do that is in bigger audiences, and the best way to bigger audiences isn't always, and perhaps isn't often, reporting on the complex political, economic or otherwise important stories. It's more appealing to a social media generation to write about celebrities, scandals and to make fun of people.

This isn't a leftist critique of the media, though it is shared with the left, but a rationalist critique of the system. A free media is absolutely necessary in a democracy, and must not be a tool of the government, otherwise it fails to be free. But if it then becomes the tool of an individual, or a financial interest, it also fails to be free. Whilst left and right governments alike have done their ideological best in ensuring the freedom of the press from government, neither has done anything to safeguard its freedom from other large interests, or to strengthen it against the capitalistic weakness it is caged by.

Partly, this is down to the conservative right's will for everything to be monetized: less regulation and as free trading as possible. Which, of course, will be backed by moguls and companies who have the same

185

will, hence they own large publishing companies to earn money. The liberal left have allowed it from a similar kind of libertarian leaning, becoming obsessed with the 'freedom' of the press, without ever realising it has forgotten that freedom means from bias interests, not just governments.

The problem exists as much today, in the social-media savvy world we inhabit, as it did 20 years ago, when newspapers ruled the roost. The 2015 UK election, for instance, saw right and left divides as usual, but the left support coming largely from the independent *Guardian*'s journalist-led approach, and the right from tabloids and broadsheets with vested interests. Which hardly seems fair, given the reliance our population has on media to inform. The resulting imbalance, as it has in almost every election for decades (except for when the political left leaned right), supported the conservative right. The Guardian posted investigative journalism about the manifesto promises, whilst the tabloids posted pictures of leftist leaders eating bacon sandwiches in an ugly manner, or the Scottish National's leader as some sort of dictatorial overlord.

What we are left with is a population of people being informed only by the interests of the people who own newspapers, and even then, only publishing stories which are immediately appealing, funny or embarrassing. People able to spin bad news, ignore important topics, and inflate the smallest things – be they pictures of breakfast, or relatively unimportant opinions. It's bizarre. We have such strict rules in politics, but arguably its most important sister – the media – goes completely unchecked in terms of its neutrality.

This is not an issue of interest solely to those on the left, or to those like me with an explicit interest in politics or economics. This is something deeply unfair and wrong at the heart of society. It's something which means our political system cannot function as it was intended to, something which throws into imbalance all of the theory that supports the idea of democracy in the first place. Democracy doesn't work in large countries full of people if the media doesn't remain neutral and free from government and personal, vested interests. That is an issue which should motivate every human being in society, regardless of political opinion, and even without a rational form of morality in place.

A media solution?

The only rational solution is to introduce checks and balances to ensure the media is functioning for society in the same way as we have so far discussed for politics. We should fund academic institutions to investigate media bias and stories, and we should – without a shadow of a doubt – give power to a rational, independent media watchdog (which is scrutinised itself – perhaps we elect the head of that watchdog, as it's that important a position) which has the power to shut down any form of media company if it is deemed to be acting out of bias or failing to uphold standards of journalistic integrity. We need to do this in order to create a world where good journalists play on a fair playing field with the bad journalists, rather than allowing the bad journalists a get out of jail free card (through sensationalised stories and 'clickbait').

This is not a terribly difficult thing to do, and many Western democracies currently attempt such watchdogs. However, due to the lack of teeth these watchdogs have, they normally only pull the media up on the most outright, blatant lies, and as a media company you have to be breaking civil and criminal law regularly to even be up with a chance of closure (as the Sun's sister newspaper the News of the World managed to do a few years ago, after the phone hacking scandal). What a rational morality calls for – perhaps more than anything else – is a media watchdog with real, sharp teeth and rational balance. Something capable of actually doing the job that a media watchdog must do in a modern society.

This has to change; we can't create any kind of functioning, effective society if the media is allowed to publish misleading, bias or poor journalism. There must be ramifications for attempts to implicitly mislead the public on important political or economic matters for financial gain, in the same way that there are ramifications for personally doing so in society: we call it fraud. We've ignored this media fraud for way too long. And, indeed, fixing the state of the media could be done without any change in the political system; it should become a priority of every progressive and truthful administration.

Chapter 9: Economics

Economics, like many other areas of government policy, is currently used as a tool for politicians to push their personal opinions and perspectives. Yet economics, as an area of study, is vast, and the information it can provide us is important.

My favoured example of economic political perspective is one highlighted especially well by the wonderful 'liberal' economist (liberal being a term he uses in his column – though, a term rationalism in politics and economics has no need for) and Nobel Prize winner, Paul Krugman. In *End this Depression Now*, a book about ending the economic recession, he attacks the British Conservative government (technically at the time a coalition with the Liberal Democrats), for their use and abuse of the logic regarding deficit cuts. With the UK deep in recession, and in a large budget deficit (money owed to banks, via public borrowing), Prime Minster David Cameron and Chancellor George Osbourne opted for a tactic of deep spending cuts in order to reduce the deficit and create what Krugman calls the 'confidence fairy'. Roughly explained, this term relates to the economic theory that by cutting the country's budget deficit, businesses will gain confidence and invest more in what they believe is a more stable economy (i.e. by hiring more staff, creating more product lines, or registering new businesses, etc.). If correct, the Conservatives would cut the budget deficit and it would automatically encourage economic growth. In turn, this would lead to higher employment (as companies invested more, and hence produced more, thus needing more employees to do so), and the circle would theoretically complete, thus leading to regenerated growth. It's a nice idea, and if you had no prior knowledge of economics – as the huge majority of voters don't – it would be compelling.

Their plan of selling this to the public didn't consist of putting this economic idea out there, though. Whether they believed the public would not understand this, or whether they believed such reasons would not stand up to economic scrutiny in the public eye, the Conservatives decided to take a different tact of promoting the policy. They likened the budget deficit to credit card debts that an individual might owe, pushing the idea that these debts need paying *now* before we can go on and accumulate wealth as a country. Perhaps even more compelling than the theory, for the non-economically interested voter: we don't understand large system economics, but we all know how credit card debt works.

The tactic was highly successful – thanks to the tabloid press and the demonization of poor people who spend beyond their limits and use credit cards – so to think the entire country is in this kind of trouble is scary. It's a smart way of creating an environment in which people agree to huge cuts in public spending (to hospitals and education, and various other vital services) which they would otherwise see as an unacceptable assault on their own interests. The Conservative use of the phrases 'living within our means' and 'balancing the books' have been essential in keeping up the pretence, by continuing with this vision of personal debt to explain their economic policy. In essence, the Conservatives have created an environment where their own ideological policies of reduced government spending and welfare (i.e. reducing the advantages for the poorer in society, as the richer don't need benefits and don't tend to use public health care) seem like the natural, sensible way out. It's ingenious, really.

However, this deficit reduction plan, which has continued through successive centre-right and right-wing governments, has yet to take the UK out of recession (even pre-covid). Given it is part of Conservative ideology to reduce public spending, a cynic might suggest it will stay long after covid has gone.

Krugman proposes that history and logic provide evidence that this policy was never an honest, workable tactic. He notes such recent failures as further evidence that we are living in a 'Keynesian' society. John Maynard Keynes noted, as early as 1936, that as economic output is strongly influenced by demand, the way we should fight a recession (when unemployment is high, and thus less people are spending – both as a necessity, by having less cash, and through a fear of the price of basic products rising) is by increasing public spending instead of decreasing it. Decreasing spending simply cuts even more demand, as there becomes less government employment and less government-bought services – such as road building contractors, hospital workers, etc. – meaning less real income in the population which can be spent. This in turn prolongs the recession by adding to the problem, or at least failing to tackle the cause, which is falling demand. The 'confidence fairy', which the Conservatives believed they were summoning by reducing a deficit and thus creating the confidence for investment, has never appeared, as companies aren't particularly motivated by the level of deficit – they are much more influenced, obviously, by how much cash consumers have to spend, how much they are willing to spend, and how much government public spending is available to get a slice of.

Of course the Conservatives did not allow us to get into this debate because they chose analogies which didn't allow for it; credit card debt does not analogise well for complex public spending debt, and so all debate was avoided in favour of simplistic arguments.

Those economists who do back Conservative financial thinking propose that because we already have a huge budget deficit, then we have already spent too much in the preceding years, and thus can't afford to be borrowing a great deal more, full stop. Yet Krugman does not stick solely with his argument that such extra deficit is necessary. He argues that they are not explaining government debt in the right way. Government debt is not some 1,000% interest short-term loan like we see with credit card debt; it is a long-term loan to help improve society. Similarly, national debt can be reduced in a variety of more effective ways that simply isn't relevant in personal debt.

Think of public debt as a huge, monumental amount of money with a relatively small rate of interest. This means that if you have five years of good inflation – i.e. where the cost of products increases by a certain percentage, most likely due to high employment, which in turn is usually the result of higher demand (which we could only affect in current society with higher public spending) – then the rate of inflation will decrease the value of money, and do so faster than the interest rate can raise the value of that particular debt. This is because the level of debt a government holds is not simply a set figure, it is relative to the GDP (gross domestic product; the total economic output of a country), so higher inflation rates in this way means higher GDP, which in turn decreases the value of the debt. So even though we may have had to

192

borrow more money to get the economy moving again (to get GDP and inflation rising), the level of debt is actually naturally reducing as the money which the debt consists of is now worth less than it was before.

If you didn't follow that, you won't be alone – we have absolutely no economic understanding through most of our media, so I'll try to provide a better analogy. Think of a farm. Imagine you have five milking cows, but you owe another farmer one of your milking cows. You can give him that cow now, and reduce your own milk stocks by 20% immediately (1 in 5). Alternatively, you can keep the debt until birthing season, when each of your cows have given birth, and maybe even a season after that, when each of those new cows have given birth, too. The interest on the debt might have doubled, as you've taken so long to pay the debt, meaning you now owe that other farmer *two* cows. However, you have now grown your collection of cows to fifteen rather than five. So your debt is only worth 13% of your wealth (2 in 15), rather than 20% (1 in 5).

Had you paid your debt of one cow immediately – which was significant and scary, remember, as it was 20% of your entire business – not only would you have paid more of your wealth than you otherwise needed to, but you would also now have fewer cows than you do; you would have had four cows reproducing, leaving you with twelve cows altogether (rather than fifteen). You were worse off when you paid the debt, and you'd be worse off now. But because you waited to pay your debt, and invested that which you could have paid as debt, you ended up with more capital and a less economically damaging debt too.

This is a great analogy for explaining the relation between debt and GDP (the total amount of money the country has). When GDP

193

is low, and things aren't great, you can stimulate a better economy by borrowing more (another cow, perhaps!). Then, when things are better, you have to pay more back, but the debt will have paid for itself if you've grown your business, or economy, in the meantime.

The analogy isn't perfect: it only works if your economy does actually increase. However, in a country where your debt isn't just one cow but the equivalent of one cow per year, it's even more relevant. Losing a cow every year is extremely damaging, if you aren't stimulating the increase in cows at all.

As you'll note, this is not like credit card debt in any meaningful way. As an individual with a credit card, you have absolutely no way to change the value of that debt, and the interest rate on it is so high that you'd have to be creating wealth at the level of Bill Gates or Mark Zuckerberg in order to reduce the value of the debt without paying it off.

This is not common sense; to turn a famous phrase, if economics was just common sense then we wouldn't need economists. But it is vitally important. A conservative policy of cuts is not just a political decision, it impacts on the lives of millions: reducing the quality of healthcare which directly impacts on the lives of the poorest, reducing the quality of education which reduces quality of life and our civilised progress; and also necessarily increasing unemployment, which is one of the most stressful and health impacting events that could happen upon any member of society. If there is another, better option, then this policy is real irrational decision-making – most probably the result of a skewed moral outlook on the behalf or right-wing politicians – which genuinely decreases the well-being of real people.

Through the use of examples like this we can argue that politicians largely pick and choose economic theory based on how well it fits their policy; after all, even the most seemingly clear cut of arguments, like those about getting the country out of huge debt, are actually fiercely debatable and not a marker that we require budget cuts. This picking and choosing is clearly untenable in a system of rational government, where such decisions should be informed against and stopped. The likes of Krugman and other Keynesian scholars would long since have analysed and publicly called for debate to oppose such huge spending cuts if our political system were better informed. So it isn't necessarily the economic system that is broken, so much as the political system that refuses to allow reason into debates of economics.

However, for the purposes of this theory we can't just start with a system of organised capitalism, like we currently have, and then make it evidence based. If we are flirting with a system of evidence-based moral values – and we know what our basic principles of human morality are – then we must also question the type of economic system we currently have as a whole. Does it even work once we've analysed the moral rules that underpin it?

Socialism

Firstly, do we need economics at all? The closest we can get to eliminating economics, whilst still having some sort of organised moral science and democratic aristocracy, would be a version of economic socialism or Marxism. In its most basic format still, this would presumably consist of a roughly agreed system of bartering and exchange of goods rather than a system of any defined currency.

We know this kind of system works in some way because it existed in societies around the world prior to the use of organised currencies. However, it doesn't seem to work particularly well in any kind of advanced, modern world. How do moral scientists, or government officials (as well as most other people in society) make a living? It seems that to return to a basic system of bartering we would need to do away with much of the industrialisation and technological development we have gone through, in exchange for trying to find individual farms or roles for people which would allow for them to create products with which to barter. And for what ends? There doesn't seem to be anything particularly irrational about a system of currency, so we aren't gaining anything useful.

Currency, at its most basic level, is just a useful tool for sharing resources without having to directly swap physical resources with one another.[100] The problems of modern capitalism – the greed, the corruption and the poverty – are not an argument against currency. We should only consider such an outdated system of bartering if every other system of economics is fatally flawed, as it is nothing more than a simple system of returning society to its more primitive roots. We want to improve society, fixing the problems of structure we have and not just

---

[100] Basic level bartering is a system which becomes obsolete once we have a wide variety of resources in which most people do not want most things. For example, if the thing I want is a sack of potatoes, but the farmer with the potatoes didn't want cans of beans – which is all I have to spare – then I'd have to spend dubious amounts of time and effort finding a network of swaps to get my potatoes in exchange for my beans. It makes more sense to simply use currency as symbols of resources, allowing us to use reason to smooth the problems of individual differences.

reversing the changes we have made. It would be too simplistic to throw the baby out with the bathwater.

A more civilised form of socialism would be a form of market socialism. This would involve systems like we currently have: currency, companies supplying the public, and the public working for companies to earn currency, whilst buying resources from companies by using some of this currency. These kinds of ideas are central to any form of economics as they allow things to interconnect: we can organise a society so that necessary tasks get done and so that everyone fairly does their bit.

Market socialism would be different to capitalism, though. There are varying degrees of market socialism, but primarily we might want to define it as the government owning the means of production, but allowing managers to run them for a limited profit. Hence we have some of the advantages of a free market when it comes to competition and profit-orientation (to a limited degree), but all profit is due to government and hence directly improves the country rather than sitting in the pockets of a small percentile of the rich (company managers receive capped salaries, unlike company directors under capitalism who receive potentially unlimited profits).

This is very appealing. A huge problem in our society is inequality, which itself is forced by an unequal distribution of wealth. It doesn't just mean that the rich can afford more holidays or bigger houses, but also that the poorest often can't afford the basics with which to live. The better kinds of market socialism allow for technological and economic development, whilst automatically distributing the wealth much more equally.

The disadvantages are fairly severe, though. How do we switch to a system of market socialism? It's another one of those anarchist-esque ideals, but how do you go about taking the life's work of the rich, or the life savings of the middle and lower middle class, and redistributing it among everyone, whilst taking state control of all companies? Whilst moral science and rational politics takes an adjustment – perhaps even a huge reorganisation – market socialism requires a government interference of totalitarian proportions. This is a fatal disadvantage to the theory. Whilst it might end up with a better system of economics afterwards, we cannot easily justify immoral actions of this proportion. In the politics section we steadfastly ruled out totalitarianism as ever being capable of making rational, moral decisions. The ignorance of our three moral principles – especially causing huge issues in fairness and protection of interests – mean this form of economics is not too appealing, as a neutral matter.

Again, this doesn't necessarily mean it isn't the best system – the question is whether or not we can amend capitalism to suit our needs and thus provide an easier option? A disadvantage such as this is only a fatal problem for market socialism if current capitalism *doesn't have* a fatal disadvantage. If capitalism necessarily results in poverty for the majority of the world, as at current, which leads to the biggest problems that society currently faces – and indeed the worst kinds of moral irrationality – then we have to rule the immorality of carrying this on indefinitely, against the immorality of a swift totalitarian switch toward market socialism. The best option would be to not force ourselves into that lesser-evil decision and find a better way.

Capitalism

Capitalism in current society doesn't work right, there's no doubt about that. We have a system in which wealth is so unevenly distributed that it causes huge moral problems. Perhaps we can go so far as to say it causes most moral problems. As already noted, it is the primary cause of poverty, which in turns leads to starvation, high infant mortality rates, low education and employment rates, higher levels of disease, and even trickles down into problems such as homelessness (with less people in the poorest classes being able to afford to live in homes), global warming (with companies being motivated by shorter term profit and not acting responsibly for the future) and animal cruelty, with people ignoring the plight of other sentient individuals whilst they struggle to find resources to stay alive; after all, do we think people willingly support factory farming for the fun of it, or do so because it is cheap and convenient to buy into? We live in a system which means most of us can't ignore what is cheap and convenient.

Furthermore, the only motivator for current capitalism is intense greed; the most successful business people will not just be financially comfortable, they will amass wealth of obscene proportions which is neither necessary nor rational. This means that currency, with which each unit theoretically refers to a unit of resources in the world, piles up in bank accounts or goes towards the expensive luxury items of the rich, whilst many poorer people, and entire nations, struggle to amass enough currency to make a living or create an able and competitive economy.

In capitalism, like in most other economic systems, resources can be bought with use of currency. That currency's worth is determined in a variety of ways, but as a fundamental matter if you have a relatively large amount of that currency you can buy easily enough resources to survive and enjoy your life, whereas if you have none then you will struggle to survive. In Western society the government often picks up the slack of capitalism in the latter case, by providing those victims of the system with welfare benefits. But in the same way that in the West we have rich people and poor people, within the world we have rich countries and poor countries. The poor countries cannot afford to pick up the slack, international aid is limited, and thus the majority of the world ends up living in poverty under the system of capitalism which we currently have. And, as earlier noted, we then see the most serious moral problems of society rear up.

Unbelievably, even the government picking up the slack is criticised by many devout worshippers of modern capitalism – some of the same people who want us to believe that national debt is analogous to credit card debt. A fair few dogmatic followers believe that if someone is unemployed then they are either lazy or stupid, and thus have no claims to our taxes; welfare being funded by taxes which we all pay when in employment, or when buying certain products. This is not just a morally inept way of looking at the poor, it is also ignorant of how capitalism works.

Capitalism requires a level of freedom being afforded to companies in which they can function more or less how they want: they are free to hire, fire and make money in any legal manner they so wish. There is no restriction unless laws are explicitly broken (and even then there are certain protections afforded to businesses in order to encourage business owners to take certain risks), and this freedom necessitates individual victims within society. If a company needs to cut costs, they are duty bound to do things like cut the number of employees before sacrificing even smaller amounts of profits. Capitalism demands that profit be put first. Similarly, in a recession, where most companies are trying to cut costs due to reduced aggregate demand, it is necessarily the case that unemployment will rise faster. Companies have to try and cut all unnecessary costs, and necessarily this means an average cut in employed people in the country.

The uncomfortable truths don't end there. For there to be any chance of a country sustaining long-term growth, there almost always needs to be a pool of unemployed people (be they nationals or immigrants). If there are no unemployed people, then how does a flourishing company grow its workforce to accommodate higher sales? It would be scuppered by a lack of an unemployment pool for the same reason that it is often scuppered when there is a lack of raw materials. Companies can grow simply by increasing revenue or profit percentages, but one of the major causes of growth is in reducing unemployment: if there is no unemployment to reduce – no unemployed people to draft in and create the extra products or services – then there's much less chance of growth. In this way, capitalism is meant to work similarly to an ecosystem: companies compete, populations of each company might grow or fall as a result, and the workers are resources which they use to grow. The availability of resources falls and grows organically as the system develops over time. Unemployment is a necessary part of this development, as people are a necessary resource, so it's not a sign of weak capitalism or lazy potential workers.

The problem we have at current is that right-wing opinion – of the type we discussed from the Conservatives at the beginning of the chapter – is squeezing the logic out of capitalism, rather than improving the system for everyone's benefit. They are finding ways of convincing the public of not just cutting public spending, but also of reducing taxes for the rich and for big companies. Even finding ways to argue that unemployed people are to blame, by hiding the logic of capitalism. But if a capitalist system stops benefitting the masses like this, it stops being a rational method of economics.

What do these political arguments in favour of this less rational version of capitalism consist of? Primarily we see the same sort of cherry-picking evidence as we saw earlier about the budget cuts. One of the big arguments in favour of balancing capitalism against the interests of most of the public is from necessity in the line of international competition. The argument goes as follows:

If we tax big companies and big earners too heavily, then they will go elsewhere and we will lose talent, thus harming our GDP (by making international companies more successful and ours less). In turn, this leads to less profit, higher unemployment, etc., and we are worse off.

This kind of argument is so compelling because it argues from the position of an expert, against our opinions as laymen; it makes us think that perhaps it is true and thus we should let the people who know what they are doing get on with it. Indeed, half the logic is sound: if international companies take over a niche that one of our companies is filling, then our GDP will be impacted, which will lead to us being worse off in the ways stated.

But the first half of the argument is not sound. It's an unproven assertion designed to scaremonger. If capitalism is like an ecosystem – which all theory more or less agrees with, as the advantage of capitalism is in development and filling niches almost organically – then no society will ever be struggling for business, as when rich people leave others will be able to crop up. Similarly, if we tax a company lightly, thereby taking very little advantage from it residing in our society, then we aren't losing a lot if it goes elsewhere. Capitalism is not advantageous for society unless each company is paying for a good deal of the public services which its employees use, at least. Under lower tax rules, companies become a drain in which society looks after the workers, who then benefit the company almost for free. These kinds of points are entirely ignored.

Think about Amazon as a telling example. By the end of 2018 it planned to have around 27,500 employees in the UK,[101] whilst the tax it pays was only around £220 million (despite making revenues here of around £10.9 billion). £220 million is a lot of money, and a government official might argue this is a huge injection into UK infrastructure. Yet, when divided even just by the number of employees it has, this is around £8,000 each. This it to cover roads, welfare benefits for the unemployed people it might eventually employ, healthcare (which is notoriously well-used by Amazon employees), state pensions, education of the employees' children…the list goes on. As one of the most profitable companies in the world, one would expect they'd be meeting the costs of the employees they use within society, and then adding a lot of value to the economy on top. Their owner, after all, is worth around £730 billion, so there's plenty of money that he's managed to amass. It's difficult to see how they are pulling their weight despite their huge profits.

So long as taxes aren't high enough that business can't make decent profits, then in general there is little reason to worry about taxing higher. Let's not forget this 'international competition' dilemma, though, as it will be approached more thoroughly later in the chapter

---

[101] https://www.bbc.co.uk/news/business-45906785

– it isn't all as simple as I suggest here (there are situations where moving abroad leads to lower costs for international competitors, and so less business for our GDP).

The argument is even stranger when it comes to talk of individuals. Banks recently received widespread criticism after leading us into recession, then demanding public spending to help them out. Further criticism came when it was discovered that the individuals in charge of these public-money-sapping companies were receiving huge payments, millions of pounds in bonuses. The reason given was if we do not pay these individuals what the market demands then they will go elsewhere, and Britain's economy will thus be worse off.

Again, this doesn't make a lot of sense. Economics is not an exact science when it comes to the banking side of things – it's a game of taking risks (which these individuals failed to do correctly, anyway). Are we saying that no one who commands only a few hundred thousand a year, rather than millions, is able to manage a national company and responsibly deal with investments? This argument relies on our ignorance. These people are not geniuses. They are human beings who happen to know about money. There's not even any evidence that they do particularly well in the positions they inhabit compared to how anyone else would do. This is a culture and market that got out of hand, not a genuine value of 'talent'. Given that economics is an academic subject, which anyone can study, the 'talent' that is being talked about can only be that these individuals are fairly bright. Yet given that they failed to do their job even partly correctly in the long term, assertions can be cast on this assumption of their vastly superior intelligence. The only other thing that can be meant by 'talent' is some ability to see the future, like a mysterious sage might. Their inability to see the economic collapse shows this not to be true, even if we renounce our scientific outlook on the possibility of psychics.

We've seen a worldwide slump in economic activity, which should, if nothing else, give confidence for taxpayers to demand more sensible pay for people in these positions. There are vast numbers of academic areas where people are expected to be highly educated, able to make predictions and then act responsibly based on evidence – all areas of science exist entirely on these guidelines, for example – those involved in finance are not above any other. If nothing else, a more moderate salary means the person receiving it has to worry about the future implications of his actions, rather than safely gambling in the knowledge that he doesn't ever have to work again if he doesn't want to.

The arguments against 'tax lightly or lose out' are easily as plausible as that which is supposed by right-wing politicians; I would argue that they are in fact much *more* plausible. If we tax too highly the individual might go somewhere else. Yet are we really that scared of our own education systems that we think this individual is miles better than anyone else in the entire country? We need to have some perspective here: we're all human beings and have roughly the same set of mental abilities. We can test for different sorts of intelligence, problem solving ability and ability to multitask. We can also teach those high performers in any academic subject, including finance and economics. Arguments for 'economic geniuses' lack perspective, or any seeming knowledge of other sciences.

Can we fix capitalism?

Given the difficulty of adopting any type of market socialism, the only thing capitalism needs to do to legitimately continue, is offer a way it could be changed to do morally as well as market socialism, and then be safeguarded to do as such (i.e. it must do more than *promise* to be better, there must also be reason and evidence on side). Of course once we introduce a similar system to rational politics – whereby economic decisions in government are made on the basis of objective economic study, and not argued based on policy or opinion – we automatically achieve an improvement.

This improvement needs to do better than simply not being a right-wing propaganda machine though, it needs to do much better. Socialism automatically redistributes wealth, so if we are not going to force state ownership of industry then we would need to change the system of capitalism to be far less greed based. We would need to increase taxes in big companies and high earners significantly – not dissimilar to a Robin Hood Tax, in essence – whereby the highest earners still earn enough to be elite (hundreds of thousands a year, perhaps with an ever increasing 5% possible rise per year after hitting an initial limit, if they are still producing enough profit to allow it) however the percentage of tax would need to keep rising to keep individuals only earning 5% more each year at the highest brackets. This extra tax revenue could reduce deficits, do away with much of the reliance on banking and debt and improve society greatly – from the improvements of health and education services, all the way through to measures which solve the energy crisis and improve the transport network.

We are talking about the reduction of billion/million-pound salaries/dividends coming down to hundred thousands and a few million at the very most; hundreds of billions of extra tax revenue added yearly. The exact figure could not possibly be known at the moment; however, we do know that 18,000 people now make £1 million a year in the UK. If we conservatively estimate that each of those would see a reduction in income of £300,000 a year (some would be less, many would be much more), which would be taken in tax, then we would see an extra £54 billion per year. Let's also consider the much larger group earning over £100,000. Around 712,000 extra people are in this bracket, which most of us would consider a sign of wealth. If we supposed that this group would only have their earnings reduced by an average of £10,000 each then that works out at £71 billion. When added to the millionaires figure we have an extra £125 billion extra per year. Nine years of this extra tax would pay off the entire national debt (estimated to be around £900 billion), even though we have already noted that this may not be the best way to deal with debt.

Yet this extra tax income is not something which the rich would be gifting to society, as the right wing think; they are services which the rich owe to society by virtue of society agreeing to a system of capitalism which rewards exactly that skill or lifestyle which has made them money in the first place. People often forget that human society doesn't and shouldn't automatically reward greed or economic ability, and thus such rewards should be removed if the system of rewards is leading to huge inequalities elsewhere. As a purely logical matter, whereby we examine economics by its very point of existence – which is to best serve all of society – we cannot find support for the opinion that the poor are unworthy benefactors of the generosity of the rich. Not without also exposing the truth that this generosity is only possible since the poor agree to live in a system whereby the rich are allowed the calculation of value which allows them to be rich in the first place. Truth is truth; it should not be ignored by any political agenda. It must be said that many of the rich do not ever make these kinds of reasonless perspective-based arguments anyway, and were politicians to be forced to stop making them then they would soon die out.

Of course the kind of policy of 'Robin Hood' taxation, which seems to be a way of equalising society, is not without its problems. It will be less effective the less countries do it, for example, so we also need to begin thinking internationally. Significant social change – and that is what improving capitalism is: social change – can rarely be achieved within only one society. We all share the world and if some societies try to take advantage of fairer rules here by providing unfair rules there which benefit their society in the meantime (by attracting higher investment), then we need to attack that problem head on. We must provide some sort of global redistribution of wealth – from our massive increase in taxes we could theoretically afford to do this – incentivising nations not to allow tax havens (either by asking them to put in place restrictions on moving business, or to have fairer tax rules themselves), and forcing change globally. Tax havens are not a difficult thing to phase out, they are simply politically complex.

There are practical ways of doing this, and the short-term fairer increase in taxes is a wonderful way to give yourself a fund to start doing it. Even if you used all of the first couple of years extra revenue only to stop further deficit cuts (and not increasing public spending in the immediate at all) then using all the spare accumulated wealth to encourage other nations to take the same system, via a hand out of loans with repayments of low interest or even of grants via foreign aid, then you have a hopeful system by which we can start international discussion.

The problems with the necessary fairer system of tax should ask us to problem solve in this kind of manner, rather than ask us to abandon it in favour of a system of capitalism which is absolutely unfit for purpose. The modern political right wing has an unexamined and seemingly unchallenged opinion that we should do the latter, but as human beings we have a moral obligation to do the former.

This kind of system of international diplomacy would not just be handy for improving the tax system in our countries, it would also allow for a rolling out of this much better system of capitalism from the richer countries to the poorer countries, with the poorer countries benefitting in ways which were only possible previously by being exploited for their cheap labour. Economics, politics and moral science all interconnect under this system, whereby poorer countries are given constant aid and economic encouragement due to a restriction in greed in wealthier nations. In turn, the lessening rate of sweatshop opportunities by wealthy foreign companies, yet continuing rate of finances via this system, will lead to poorer nations having vastly increased economic opportunities for domestic entrepreneurs. So almost incidentally, in theory we have also provided a framework for improving and providing a much-required boost for poorer and developing countries to take up a fair and sustainable version of capitalism. Nowhere would be required to force themselves into tax havens or sweatshop economies.

There is one final possible outcome of this kind of system, and it is not a minor one. The potential for economic collapse is greatly lessened. This is because profits are more tightly taxed, individuals are restricted by maximum wages and international connections are both strengthened and secured. Of course this is not an automatic consequence: we would still need to ensure that governments are run sensibly (which, by gradually switching to a democratic autocracy, we are in the best position to do) and no doubt there will be masses of road bumps along the way. What we must learn from the ideas herein is not that this system is perfect or faultless, but rather that problems and challenges can be solved without resorting to easy and counter-productive answers. Currently this is how we try to solve economic problems; we plump for right-wing answers; for greed over rationality; for laziness over critical thinking. The path to better systems can't possibly be forged this way. We must be open to solving issues with new ideas rather than plumping for unacceptable old ones.

Interconnection

The current economic landscape is not necessarily the way it is because people believe it is rational; for the most part, it seems fair to hypothesise that a stunted moral opinion is causing the majority of the problems. A non-autocratic and non-qualified system of democracy means that we do not do what is fair, or what is rational, but rather what we are most easily persuaded to by often shady or easily influenced politicians. Freeing ourselves of this flawed political structure is the first step in any improvement, and this is the bit that can be done without international change. Setting a successful precedent for making this political change in any large, civilised society will undoubtedly provide a rational catalyst for widespread change.

In turn this can help to move us away from the right-wing politics and economics that keep most of us firmly rooted in the relative dark ages. Internationally, our new system of politics would also provide us with genuinely educated and able proponents of the systems and theories which we are choosing: the best people for the job of persuading other people around the world of taking the journey with us. The system of rational politics and rational economics are interconnected in a way which they absolutely have to be, resulting in a stronger system as a whole. As a small side note, if you are explicitly turning towards rationality, you are also explicitly turning towards an inward-looking system that, one would hope, could better spend the taxes we already make. We will not have departments run by people with biases and personal ideologies, they will be run by people of experience and ability. And not by short term administrations, but by accountable, long-term responsible officers – where change happens when it is rational to do so, and not when the government changes every four years. It is difficult not to foresee this as an eventual ideal in being most effective with our taxes.

Strength through connection

The interconnected strength allows us to use an improved form of capitalism as our blueprint for a better world. But this in turn is only possible if we can satisfy a set of necessary goals. We need to create an economy in which the rich pay a much higher, ever increasing percentage of tax, whilst the poor pay little to none; hitting psychological maximums so as both the poorer and the rich are motivated equally for success, whilst safeguarding against the kind of reward system that creates moral inequalities. We also need to ensure that we plan for international collaboration and prepare to have to persuade, and financially support, the closing of tax havens and the rehabilitation of international nations. Last, but by no means least, we need to educate people on the point of economics.

211

Economics isn't a natural science: the world isn't naturally geared toward rewarding greed or business risk, whilst punishing/ignoring those with no economic ambition. It is this way only because it is deemed the best way to serve the people, and to organise trade and society. We have reached a stage where the majority of the world is in poverty, and in which even Western societies are seeing a massive, growing division between the rich and the poor (funded by a growing class of poor people). This means that capitalism is not currently fit for purpose, and our choices are thus rationally limited to authoritarian socialist intervention, or else improved, fairer capitalism. I have opted for the latter option, as I believe capitalism is improvable and that authoritarian decisions are shown by history to be untenable and unacceptable.

Yet both of these systems (fair capitalism and market socialism) share the strengths of capitalism: the ability to motivate and the ability to forge technological progress which improves society even further. If we do not change capitalism in a significant manner, using all of the theory and evidence at our disposal to push it onto safeguarded, working tracks, then it is difficult to see how we can justify social change which does not involve socialism of the type I have mentioned.

Humans are not perfect rational machines and we are biased by greed and selfishness, which is instilled in us by an evolutionary process that has also imprinted us with emotions of guilt and empathy. If capitalism cannot rationally overcome its propensity for increasing and dealing only in greed, then we must abandon it in favour of a better system, where profits of industry are never seen as belonging to anyone but society itself. I don't envisage that capitalism is unworkable in this way; I don't think that it necessarily grows greed. I believe that we didn't develop capitalism as careful and concerned citizens, always aware of its purpose, and instead allowed ourselves to be carried away with this feeling of entitlement it gave to the rich as it grew over centuries. It is time that we examined where we have gotten to, what problems we need to deal with and what solutions need enacting now. It's time for critical reflection on capitalism and necessary change. Rational economics is within our grasp.

Chapter 10: The Changing Face of Ethics and Society

What We Are

It is easy to look back over the ages and plot the remarkable moral development of humans. From an evolutionary point that saw us develop from lower primates with limited intellect, we have created societies that strive to value equality and fairness; achieving great technological steps and feats of science, alongside a more than equally great moral journey that has included the abolition of slavery based on race, sex and age, the protection of the young and the vulnerable, and the outlawing of many violent and societally disruptive acts. This is an impressive list for a bunch of apes.

Of course we can trace the moral characteristics of societies of ants, or vampire bats, but the ability to be able to survive without helping others, whilst still making the choice to do so is what truly sets human beings apart. We see rare instances in nature of altruism, but nothing like in the examples we can pool from the human species. Were a technologically and intellectually advanced alien race to happen upon Earth tomorrow, it is surely this moral ability that they will note sets us apart from other animals.

This is not to denigrate our scientific achievements. Quite on the contrary. Powered by stuff we dug up from the ground, and consisting of nothing but things we found lying around, we have managed to create rockets capable of flying us into space and landing on that tiny pale dot in the night sky. More impressively, we can now reach the almost invisible red dot even further away, and program a robot to suss it out for us. And this is just in one tiny area of science. We've also created vaccines capable of halting intelligent viruses, cobbled together machines which can in hours compute equations that it might otherwise take a brilliant mathematician his whole career to do, built towering skyscrapers sturdy and clever enough to withstand earthquakes which we've never even experienced (just in case), and written theories and systems smart enough to work out the weather before it even happens. These are things to be genuinely proud and in awe of.

And yet my human pride in these achievements is nothing compared to the pride of being a member of the same species of the great moral heroes from history, who showed that humans could do something even greater: sacrifice genetic desires in favour of doing what's right. People like Emily Davison, who so passionately believed in women's rights that she threw herself under the king's horse at the Epsom Derby in protest, fully aware of the fatal injuries she might, and indeed did, receive. Or Frederick Douglass, a former slave who escaped and spent his life (and not to mention his wonderful oratory and literary ability) supporting the cause of abolition. Or how about Charles Darwin who – initially unwittingly, perhaps – fought everything he was in order to provide the truthful basis of the ideas which have freed us all from the emancipation of religion.

Darwin wasn't an atheist desperate to prove his beliefs, but a man struggling with truths which were changing his and everyone else's views, making him feel isolated from his beloved family. In 1839 his wife, Emma, wrote a touching letter to him, probably trying to lovingly persuade him that his discoveries don't have to impact upon his faith. In it she included the following sentence:

Your mind & time are full of the most interesting subjects & thoughts of the most absorbing kind, viz following up your own discoveries — but which make it very difficult for you to avoid casting out as interruptions other sorts of thoughts which have no relation to what you are pursuing... I agree with you almost if not quite. I do not wish for any answer to all this — it is a satisfaction to me to write it & when I talk to you about it I cannot say exactly what I wish to say, & I know you will have patience, with your own dear wife.

Some time later, Charles wrote the following note at the end of a returning letter:

When I am dead, know that many times, I have kissed & cryed over this. C. D.

Perhaps this is an unknown part of Darwin's story, but it is one of personal bravery, emotional anguish, moral courage and the kind of heroism which most of us will likely never have to know. Yet, perhaps unlike the legendary status of Davison and Douglass, it is the kind which we would all like to think we are capable of.

As humans we are built to create leaps in technology, as it is that which provides us greater comfort or greater ability to reproduce our genes safely. And yet the leaps we want in moral terms are an awful lot more dangerous, and an awful lot less safe. It is this courage to close our eyes and leap based on rational, moral ideas which truly sets us apart as a remarkable species. We are braver than any of those pre-hominid apes could possibly have imagined. We are often braver than we – even today – imagine.

216

Perhaps it is because we look with such admiration at the likes of Davison or Douglass – or even Darwin – that we now feel rather powerless about developing ethics any further. Perhaps we look at the great leaps we have made and think 'We've already gotten there'. Or perhaps, as I stated at the very start, we tend to believe that without a religious viewpoint there are no black and white moral causes any more.

This book was written with the aim of deleting that last theory; without God, morality is still alive and well. Moreover, without God morality is *better* because it can be consistent and not arbitrarily decided based on mythical rules. And yet the former two beliefs are also false: we have a lot to be proud of in terms of morality, but we are certainly *not* there yet. In Davison's culture and in Douglass's culture there were times when the majority of people believed that these kinds of social changes were actually 'extreme' or pointless because 'we had already gotten there' when it came to perfecting ethics. No society thinks it is currently morally wrong, or going to develop any further, instead *every* society sees itself as the pinnacle of morality. We are no different, and we are no less wrong.

A different kind of ethics, for a different kind of world

It is this realisation – that we are no different from other societies in thinking we are morally perfect – that no doubt spurred an eventual change in moral code throughout the ages. But it is clear that for us to progress we must make one further realisation in our modern, economically organised society: heroic acts are no longer necessarily the result of direct action or bravery in the face of aggression. Undoubtedly it is these kinds of revolutions around the world that grab the headlines,

217

and yet effective development and progression primarily comes in the form of personal responsibility and courage of a different kind.

We live in societies, for instance, where paying taxes is a moral obligation on behalf of those who have money (to help provide social services such as healthcare and the education system), and yet tax avoidance isn't technically illegal (plenty of loopholes exist, if you want to find them). We also live in societies where the largest amount of violence isn't on the streets and being aimed at strangers or enemies, but hidden away in family homes and supported by the sexual objectification of women, or else perpetrated against members of other species to satisfy our dining norms. In essence, our greatest moral obligations are no longer necessarily in formal protest or direct action, but take the forms of choosing not to exploit the tax system, or choosing not to support sexist ideas about women's roles, or choosing not to buy products of immense suffering by the individuals of other species. Those on the right of politics may have demonised these as 'lefty' or 'communist', but they aren't, they are rational. If the right is about greed, and the left is about bleeding hearts, we should also choose to stand in the middle – neither left, nor right, nor even centrist – but rationalists, making decisions that are not dogmatic, but correct and evidence-based.

This might seem simple and easy compared to the struggles of Davison and Douglass, but moral problems still require a certain bravery to push them forwards; a bravery we should revere and be proud to stand up for. It is not easy, for example, to be a young male and to choose not to bow to peer pressure in objectifying women. It is not easy to be an educated business person (judged upon their ability to maximise profits) and not to seek the avoidance of tax. It is not easy to be a functioning member of a society that routinely provides the products of animal exploitation, whilst refusing to eat and wear what everyone else does. These examples do not require the bravery of a slave fleeing a plantation and opposing his oppressors, or a woman facing death to further the rights of other women, but they still require a bravery for which you will likely never be applauded; a bravery to do what's right, without promise of recognition. Perhaps even a bravery not just to do what's right, but to talk to others about doing it.

Yet this is what ethics in the modern world looks like. Remember the guy who chucked himself in the river at the Oxford–Cambridge boat race in 2012, to protest elitism? No? Or you do, but don't see him in the quite same light as Emily Davison? Well, that's exactly my point. Even if the swimmer in question had a perfectly valid argument and protest, we now have a media which is wielding norms so wide-reaching that it is tailor-made to neutralise any such perceived aggressive counteraction against societal views. People want to be comfortable, and media helps us to normalise with one another. Direct action is incredibly easy to outcast, and incredibly difficult to turn back once outcast. A change in ethics in this era will come from intelligent, respectful exchanges, and responsible, honest choices, else it won't come at all. Evidence can be found by looking at a surviving, all encroaching system of animal agriculture, in contrast to the continually jailed and pariah-labelled masked-intruders who broke in to rescue animals.

This is also where the weakness of mine, and every other moral theory in history, becomes relevant. No matter how well argued, or how well intentioned your ideas are, you can't make people act. And yet I find there is cause for greater optimism. This isn't a form of ethics like those I discussed in the first chapter; those theories which ask us to adhere to ideas which are, essentially, made up. This is a real, societally reflective theory of ethics, and it's one which we can all understand the reasons for and honestly hold to be true. That is monumentally important, at least in my opinion.

Why? Because if history teaches us anything about ethics, it's that only when the majority understand a moral movement will it become accepted. A moral theory which cannot be understood, or related back to reality (instead relying on powerful intuitions, or authority figures) can also therefore not hope to be successful in changing the state of things for the long haul. One might get short-term obedience, but it just won't stick. The fact that rational morality is a scientific way of judging and understanding morality gives great reason to believe that it can be practically successful where no other theory could. Far from us needing to indulge ancient religions as a method of socially controlling people, rational ethics give us a chance to have real, effective forms of morality.

Conclusion

Rational ethics give us three principles, upon which all of our current moral beliefs are rightly or wrongly drawn: the desire to be free/autonomous, the desire to have our important interests protected, and the desire to be treated fairly. When we return moral opinions back to these basics, I have tried to show that we can create much more rational political and economic systems, to gradually move us away from broken party politics, or unexamined and wildly unsuccessful versions of capitalism.

I have also argued that this kind of rational view of morality implicitly implores us to accept a set of truths in order to help better society: a disagreement with unchallenged systems of faith (whilst respecting personal rights to have religious belief), an acceptance of determinism (that punishment should be rehabilitative and not just punishing), and a recognition that many non-human animals are indeed subjects of a life and so deserve our respect in not being used as property, even if nothing else.

Ironically, these are the easy bits. Our move to a new political system, of gradual and slight changes to our form of capitalism, and to a slight reorganisation of our eating habits (by removing animals) and justice system (by improving rehabilitation) is actually not hugely difficult. There are many challenges, as discussed, but change doesn't happen overnight and the challenges are all surmountable.

What's more difficult, and what we may never get easy answers to, are the minutiae of political debate. A more rational version of politics helps with the big debates of our day, perhaps, by seeing immigration and international cooperation more rationally, or by making healthcare more effective. But how does one weigh up the three core principles of rational moral code when they conflict in the strongest terms? Perhaps we aren't speaking about currently contentious topics like gun control in the US, where protection and freedom for most might well outweigh freedom and perceived protection/fairness for gun owners. But undoubtedly there will be much less obvious solutions to dilemmas that will occur, and it's on these that a theory of rational ethics will really be put to the test. Yet, I'd much rather be governed by someone who was unsure but at least using the right tools for the job, than someone certain and yet acting from delusion or dogma.

CPSIA information can be obtained
at www.ICGtesting.com
Printed in the USA
BVHW071804030222
627757BV00008B/1465